APPLIED GRAPHOLOGY

How to Analyze Handwriting

BY

IRENE MARCUSE

ANATOLIA PRESS — NEW YORK

1945

This book is dedicated to the many earnest students with whom it has been my privilege to work.

CONTENTS

PREFACE

The object of this book is to present some of the modern technique which is used to make correct analyses of handwriting.

Scientific graphology now maintains a respected place in psychological research. There is an increasing realization that graphology is a dependable means of revealing the essential traits of character to such a degree that the results can be used to determine honesty or dissimulation, strength or weakness of character. Graphology detects aptitudes for vocations as well as the essence of the personality.

From the vast collection of samples of handwritings which I have assembled in many countries, and through my study and experience, I have proof of the similarity in any language of man's expression of character.

My experience as a vocational counselor in schools and as an advisor in criminal investigation has added to my wide collection of signatures and specimens of various types of handwriting. I have made tests of personality where such analysis has been required in social psychology ranging from the normal to the abnormal.

It is through such investigation and experience as mine in the past century that graphology has at last been accepted as a science.

There have been several books of importance published in the past twenty years, but the circulation has been comparatively small; therefore few people are aware that graphology is a science rather than an amusement. Graphology can be used successfully in many branches of human endeavor.

And it is with this book that I want to awaken interest in possibilities of Graphology in determining character, and guiding latent talents or abilities into suitable channels.

It is for this purpose that I am publishing some of my specimens of handwriting and their analyses so that you can see for yourself the aid graphology can be for all types and their conditions. Through graphology we can weigh the plus and minus aspects of character, and through the aspects revealed, a person can be guided on to the right road for success in this business of living.

IRENE MARCUSE

INTRODUCTION

It has been my privilege and pleasure over a number of years to be a co-worker as well as a student of Irene Marcuse, the author of this book. Through this association I am in a position to know that the material herein will be of great value to all students of graphology and an inspiration to those who are already experienced analysts of handwriting.

The author has had a wide experience as an analyst and as a vocational counselor on the Continent and in this country. There is a wealth of instructive material in her unique examples of various types of handwriting, and her constructive and psychological analyses thereof.

Through my collaboration with Irene Marcuse doors of knowledge have been opened for me in the field of graphology which had hitherto been closed, as my studies of the subject had been solely in English. This statement does not mean to imply that we do not have some good text books written in English; we have a few excellent ones, but it is well known that the most extensive works on this subject have been written in the French and German languages. Fortunately some of these books are available in this country, and it is from them that I have received the greater part of my tutelage under Irene Marcuse. She has very generously given me access to her library and her vast collection of handwritings written in many languages: and it is through these specimens from many lands one can find the proof of the equality of man clearly demonstrated. The characteristics of a man can be detected, regardless of race, creed or color through the singularity of his handwriting. It is true that every language has its national individuality of script, but in graphology we find all races have a common heritage.

It is through the discovery of these common traits in all races that a knowledge of the character of all men can be detected regardless of intents to deceive. Dependability of character is always important, and this science which reveals the character is of great value to business men both large and small who wish to hire the right types for certain positions. The ability to know better those we live close to aids in harmonizing home life. It is with the knowledge of the benefits of graphology that I can proudly endorse the contents of this book with deepest gratitude to the author for her assistance in enlarging my understanding of the subject.

For those who know little of the background of graphology, I will try to indicate some of the high points of this science. The claims now made by modern graphologists have met the critical approval of men of academic and learned societies. Therefore it is not surprising that the constantly increasing interest shown by the American public in character analysis as interpreted by handwriting has been the stimulus for this book. Its aim is to demonstrate the benefits of graphology and to acquaint the public with the importance of its usage. All analyses herein are made from scientific and psychological conclusions.

In this introduction it will be well to clear up some of the puzzling impressions the public has in general of the usage of graphology. In the first place a scientific analysis is not made through intuition or simple surmise, but upon the principles which have already passed the stage of mere observation. Although intuition does play a certain part in graphology, just as it does in all analyses, we do not accept it or let it influence us in our interpretations until after our scientific work has been validated. Stress must be laid on the fact that predictions are not made in graphology. However, it is not denied that extraordinary and penetrating deductions can be made by those who are particularly gifted with an innate talent in judging character from handwritng. It is to those people we owe the first interpretations of graphology. Serious students and doctors have amassed a collection of drawings and handwritings as evidence of certain factors repeating themselves in handwriting, and it is through their investigations and wide experience that the claims of graphology are truly justified.

To inform those who are unfamiliar with the necessary attributes for a graphologist and how his analyses are made, I will briefly outline some of the requirements. In the first place a good graphologist must have an understanding of human nature and its complexities and a delicate perception of the manner in which adjustments can be made from resultant facts. He must be a natural psychologist, and generally speaking he is far better equipped if he has studied psychology as we are aqcuainted with it today. He must be sincere and have an honest desire to patiently work out the subtleties which lie behind each speciment of handwriting. He must guard all confidences written and verbal with religous discretion.

For his physical equipment the graphologist should have an adequate specimen of handwriting executed in ink, a magnifying glass and a scheme of study to cover all the signs in the specimen such as: pressure, angle, regularity, spacing, height, width, finals, letters, words, groupings, etc.

You may ask, "What is an adequate specimen of handwriting for a character analysis?" It can be a few lines written in ink with the signature if possible, and a group of numerals as '1,2,3,4,'. . .. or for instance '20 to 30' inclusive. The age and sex of the writer should be stated.

The above mentioned would be a small specimen, but an expert graphologist can make an analysis from a surprisingly small amount of writing. It is easily understood that the more material he has to work from, the more it will facilitate the analysis. An ideal example to work from is: a letter in ink of one or more pages with signature and the addressed envelope, in which the letter is enclosed, and any other documents of the writer which have been written over a period of years in order to make comparisons of the graphic growth or deterioration of the writer.

Parents should keep specimens of their children's hand-

3

writing through their school years. It is very interesting even for the layman to note the definite changes in the writing of children at certain periods, and certainly valuable if one cares to have an analysis made for vocational guidance.

Handwriting is mind writing and we work from that principle. Can there be any doubt as to its value?

Handwriting containing constructive traits, clearly indicates the making of a good citizen, and when we find the opposite characteristics in the writing of a child or employee we know that they need help to make adjustments for a productive life. This is the aim of graphology.

SOME OF THE USES OF GRAPHOLOGY

It may surprise you to learn that there are many influential business and professional men who are aware of the benefits derived through the services of a graphologist. They employ this method to help determine in what department the applicant for employment would be best suited to work. The misplacing of able people who are perhaps temperamentally unsuited for certain situations has led to such discord and expense in organizations that it has been recognized advisably to determine beforehand the psychological adaptability of the new employee, as well, as his efficiency, for the particular position to be filled.

Many personnel managers now demand applications to be made in handwriting. Credit managers find graphology a simple means to gauge honesty. Parents, teachers, social workers, and lawyers use graphology to discover the abilities of those they are advising and trying to place in productive vocations.

All kinds of domestic, personal and business problems can be adjusted through the application of graphology, which gives you a positive knowledge of yourself and others.

Graphology is a means of determining the suitability of men and women for each other in married life. It is wise to try and discern the character and temperament of a future

4

mate while there is time to make adjustments before marriage. Many unhappily married couples turn to graphology to help solve misunderstandings, which might have been avoided if they had had a better understanding of the other's character and temperament before marriage.

Graphology definitely cannot predict whether any individual will commit a crime or even suicide. However, it can detect to a certain degree, the proneness toward criminal acts, or suicide, especially in collaboration with neurology and psychiatry.

There are certain recognized graphological signs that can be found in psychosis. There is, for instance, a very characteristic disconnection within single letters, a smeariness or blurring, which is symptomatic of general paresis, and there are, finally, signs of a pathological tempo of the impulses, which will be discussed in the chapter on mental diseases. By research and the close study of thousands of different handwritings it has been proven to furnish sure and decisive evidence whether there are pathological indications in the writing.

In the past thirty years great progress has been made in establishing graphology as a science. This has been done by W. Preyer, a child psychologist, G. Meyer, a psychiatrist, and L. Klages, a philosopher, who gave graphology a recognized place in the modern world.

THE HISTORY OF GRAPHOLOGY

In the history of graphology we find a long line of brilliant names who have shown a keen interest in the analysis of character through handwriting: Robert and Mrs. Browning, Madame De Staël, Baudelaire, Goethe, Disraeli and our own Edgar Allen Poe, They were amateurs groping in the dark, drawing their conclusions from their own interpretations and aesthetic sense. It was through such minds as these that the truth was revealed about what lay behind the characteristics shown in handwriting.

5

Through the history of the growth of the analysis of handwriting, there was an ever increasing number of erudite men around 1830, in France, including Bishops and Cardinals. Among them was Abbé Flandrin who became the teacher of the gifted Abbé Hypolite Michon. Michon possessed an extraordinary gift built on innate talent in the observation of truths that lie within handwriting. He collected, arranged, and made investigations into vast quantities of handwritings. Through his efforts and discoveries of traits in handwriting, the history of the subject really has its beginning. It was Michon who coined the word graphology.

By this time there were more than a few serious minds who devoted their efforts to satisfying what they felt could be proved truths revealed in handwriting analysis. And in the latter part of the ninteenth century the Italian criminologist Cesare Lombroso used handwriting extensively in his investigations. In France another criminologist, Alphonse Bertillon, used graphology as well as his methods of measurements as a means of identification.

Crépieux-Jamin of the French School had a contemporary in Germany named Dr. Ludwing Klages. It was he who brought the philosophical and psychological aspects into handwriting, and who used graphology to demonstrate the expression of the personal motive which has resulted in the present graphological method now recognized and used in Europe as a psycho-diagnostic instrument. His followers have amplified and refined his methods: but it was Klages who made the great and progressive step wherein graphology has grown into a study of the relation of ones handwriting to the whole picture of the person.

As time goes on there is an endless bridge of brilliant minds who carry on the work which has been done in the cause of graphology. For English reading people some of the finest books have been written by Robert Saudek. He gained his knowledge of graphology on the Continent and brought it to England where he wrote, practiced, and dem-

6

onstrated the worth of graphology as a means of discerning character and characteristics of man through his handwriting. George E. Doran of New York published some of Saudek's works, where they can still be ordered.

There is another author in England, Hans Jacoby, who has given us some of the best books written in English on graphology. Jacoby's works contain many specimens of handwriting with analyses of specimen-samples demonstrating what can be done with graphology to help solve human relations.

In America we have some excellent text on the interpretation of handwriting by Louise Rice, De Witt Lucas, Nadya Olyanova and others. To return to the name of Ludwig Klages who since about 1897 has made many discoveries about handwriting through his investigations, establishing a respected place for graphology in the psychological world, and attracting many brilliant minds as followers, among them the well known Swiss graphologist Max Pulver.

Pulver enlarged and modernized the graphological findings of Klages through applying the psycho-analytic concept in his analyses of handwriting. He was an assistant to the famous psychologist Carl Jung, in Switzerland, with whom he worked in his psycho-analytic researches by analyzing the handwritings of the patients during treatment, which proved to be a great help in determining how far the treatment been successful.

Of greatest importance for the science of graphology has been the investigation of economic crimes as outlined and discussed in Pulver's book: "Criminal Instincts in Handwriting." Through his penetrating analyses of the handwriting of internationally known financial criminals he proved the practical importance of graphological collaboration in cases of embezzlement and industrial crimes. Irene Marcuse, one of Pulver's best known disciples, continues in this line. She has been called upon in the investigation of crimes which have been committed in large banking and

7

industrial concerns and in the offiices of commercial houses.

Irene Marcuse has lectured in Italy at the Psychological Institute of Florence and Rome University. She was also invited to address the Congress of the Psychological Society about crime as detected through handwriting. In New York Irene Marcuse pursues her profession as a graphologist, lecturer and teacher, and as an analyst for personnel managers, and as a vocational counselor.

In conclusion, I wish to say, if this book arouses your interest, with its new paths of investigation I am sure you will want to pursue this study further. I know that some day the science of graphology will be applied by all thoughtful men toward success in human endeavor.

RUTH HAMPTON

CHAPTER ONE

THE TECHNIQUE OF MODERN GRAPHOLOGY

It is known that there are no two handwritings which are perfectly alike because of the simple reason that there are no two people alike. This chapter will show differences of such a high degree that one sample cannot be mistaken for another. Naturally many similarities will be noticed in handwritings of people who have similar characteristics in their personalities, but all samples deviate from each other.

After ascertaining the type and quality, the hardness or softness of the pen, we are able to learn the amount of genuine pressure. Clearly understand, therefore, that a genuine pressure can be heavy or light and realize that a genuine pressure results from the writer's own strength.

First of all, the natural and proper place for the application of pressure is in the downstrokes; the varying pressure of this downstroke movement expresses the core of the personality. Displaced pressure means that the pressure is applied in the side strokes or even the up-strokes, and those are the places in which it does not belong according to psycho-physical energy. This displaced pressure is graphically transposed from the downstrokes to the side-stroke which means psychologically that the ego is directed away from itself to the objective impulse.

The genuine pressure is a dynamic phenomenon; the heavy pressure produced by a broad pen is a mechanical one. The measure for the genuine pressure is gained by the difference between light and heavy strokes. There is a deeper meaning for pressure than will-power; the significance of pressure has its roots in profounder causes than in mere manifestations of will-power. It has a creative function, known in psycho-analytical expression as "libido".

By libido we mean all our mental and physical energies driving us to activity. This is used in two connotations:

physical	*mental*
sexuality	*intensity*

HEAVY PRESSURE

Sample 1. Generally manual workers write with heavy pressure, as do other men of great physical strength, great vitality, energy and activity, such as sportsmen and professional athletes. In addition to these, passionate writers endowed with creative minds exhibit heavy pressure. Heavy pressure is also caused through excitement and depression.

LIGHT PRESSURE

The qualities manifested by the heavy pressure are lacking in the people who write with a slight or very light pressure, almost pressureless. The light or poor pressure in handwriting shows a lack of sensual urge. It is pale and without depth. The third dimension and the libido are hardly expressed. Sexual desire is weak or absent and there is no natural driving power. In such a pressure the spiritual qualities may dominate. There is an indifference towards material desires.

Light pressure does not necessarily indicate a weak character, but when the character is weak we find a person who is easily influenced and of a fearful and timid nature. When weak pressure is accompanied by minus or poor traits, such as irregular and uneven pressure, we find an unstable person. Light pressure with accompanying plus or good traits can be the handwriting of a fine character with interests on the mental and spiritual side rather than with normal interest in material matters.

Sample 2. Light pressure indicates little impulse for combating life, a minimum of material desires for food and drink. Such a writer is not prone to demonstrate much energy; any kind of exertion does not attract him, he wants to fit in without struggle or any desire of overcoming obstacles. Light pressure is often obvious in the writings of

10

invalids and those physically exhausted; convalescents and anemics may have light pressure temporarily. These are cases where a person is confined to his bed through disability, as from an accident. This type of "shut in", may retain his original pressure slightly diminished after many years of inactivity.

PASTY PRESSURE

Sample 3. A pasty pressure is an equal pressure in up and down strokes. A pasty pressure has no shadings. A pasty pressure, when heavy, looks like a dark stream of paste as when squeezed out of a hole the size of a pinpoint from a tube of paint. The so-called pasty pressure is used by people who are easily impressed by everything that stimulates and activates the senses. We find it in the handwriting of artists and those who are impressed by rich colors. People who are sensual in their personal lives and those who are lazy and indolent, write with a pasty pressure. The latter write slowly, and perhaps without any individuality displayed in the script. The writer with pasty pressure will never leave the sensual world in favor of the spiritual one. He acknowledges the power of all sensual instincts and is easily prone to overemphasize the materialistic world. Regarded from this standpoint he is more related to the writer with heavy pressure. We can speak here of a libido which penetrates each single element of his nature. Therefore the artist finds his expression in the pasty pressure.

UNEVEN AND WAVERING PRESSURE

Sample 4. The uneven and wavering pressure shows indecision, unequal will-power, often there may be disturbances of the glands and digestive organs, or poor blood circulation may be the cause of this pressure. There is a lack of any purpose in life and a tendency to worry. The writers of this pressure are changeable, unreliable, and have little endurance; they are generally prone to petty jealousies and suspicion.

11

This uneven and wavering pressure is often found in the writing of those who are in the period of puberty and menopause. And also in the writing of unfortunate abnormal individuals. It is especially necessary to know the exact age of the writer in this case, although we always have to know the approximate age in any case of an analysis. The writer may be in the period of unrest as the result of the change from youth to maturity, or passing through the later change of life.

PERIODIC PRESSURE

Sample 5. Periodic pressure and the sudden pressure on an occasional stroke: This pressure discloses irritability and emotional unbalance. A violent nature sometimes lies behind the pressure which suddenly becomes deep, as plunging into the paper, or as in a brutal stroke. The graphologist must determine this periodic pressure from accompanying signs which we shall discuss in a later chapter. This periodic pressure is also a sign of sexual excitement in the very passionate types.

SMEARY AND MUDDY PRESSURE

Sample 6. Physical weariness and various organic disturbances may be the cause of a smeary and muddy pressure. Alcoholism and drug-addiction may be expected in a smeary and muddy pressure.

Psychotics often display such pressure accompanied by oddities and startling movements in the handwriting.

HORIZONTAL OR DISPLACED PRESSURE

Sample 7. At the begining of this chapter we learned that the proper place for the application of pressure is in the downstroke. The word "displaced" is an explanatory one for the displaced pressure. Through experience we have found that the displaced pressure introduces extreme complications for even the experienced graphologist. We must be cautious about drawing conclusions from horizontal pressure.

Displaced pressure means that the pressure is applied

in the side stroke or even in the upstroke. Those are the places where it does not belong according to the action of psycho-physical energy.

Generally this pressure is a sign that the libido or all our vital energies which drive us to activity is directed more towards an active than to a sensual life. It indicates an overpowering urge towards a goal which must be satisfied. The desire to gain power and success is increased, while sexuality becomes less important.

In this case the displacement shows that the sex energy is directed towards a creative plan or pattern in an all-engrossing expression, kindled with passion and directed towards a creative work. The sex energies are displaced for a creative expression of fulfillment. This is the constructive side of the displaced pressure.

On the negative side, we find that the displaced pressure means that sex energies are perverted and abnormal. It is not strange then, that we find displaced pressure in the handwriting of those whose sex energies are misplaced. However, the psychological interpretation of this pressure is only to apply as misplaced sex energies when it coincides with other graphic characteristics which will be explained in the chapter concerning abnormalities.

BASIC LINE

The basic line varies. It may be steady (S.1) or wavering; (S. 6) it may slope upward or downward; and sometimes it drops dramatically.

Unless there is a marked tendency off the steady basic line we may consider it as steady. When in doubt, we have to turn the page upside down; this is the best way to detect the basic line.

Sometimes the direction of the whole writing is upward or downward. This may be from placing the paper in a wrong position, causing the basic line to be directed upward or downward. Sometimes eye-strain compels the writer to write in an extreme direction upward. Again,

13

the upward direction may be attributed to a genuine tendency towards optimism.

The falling line may be attributed to extreme depression.

Sometimes a determined downward slope of the basic line coincides with the characteristics of a heavy-pressure writer, as in a nature which will not leave a stone unturned to gain its object.

REGULARITY

Absolute regularity cannot be found in any writing for the simple reason that it is produced by a living being. We may, however, speak of a relatively greater or lesser regularity of the writing movement.

Sample 1. Shows a degree of regularity, which means that up and down strokes are equal and the basic line is steady.

In regularity of the movements of the pen a capacity for work and concentration is disclosed. An equal height and width of letters gives evidence of perseverance, physical resistance, diligence, self-control, and consistent energies. However, regularity also is frequently a characteristic of poor impressionability and apathy.

Regular writing coupled with angularity shows indifference and a lack of sensibility. Often there is a rigid regularity exhibited in the writings of priests, monks, and nuns, and in that of persons who are obliged to live a severely disciplined life. Rigid and regular writing coupled with a leftward slant often reveals deceitful characters, imposters, defrauders or forgers. These individuals carry a mask over their turpitude. They must appear extraordinarily correct, therefore the right regularity in their writing is almost a symbol of deceit, a sheep's clothing thrown over the wolf. S. 89.

IRREGULARITY

A certain irregularity appears in sample 83. We see that, the angle of up and downstrokes is extremely oscillating coupled with a continuous change of slant.

Sample 4. Irregular writing together with uneven pressure:

14

This shows nervous sensibility and a nature open to impressions and excitement. Sensitive people who are easily impressed, and as easily exhausted, generally write in this fashion.

Unequalness of graphological traits may signify either a variety of ideas, or weakness of character. The artist and the intellectual almost always write an unequal hand. We notice unequalness in the handwriting of unstable characters and neurasthenics, in both of whom the energies are unbalanced.

SLANT IS THE INDICATOR OF THE EMOTIONS

Sample 7. The rightward slant in handwriting discloses initiative, activity, and an interest in world and action. When this is coupled with simplified letters, it reveals an objective mind. An easy-to-approach writer reveals himself in this slant; his active ideas must be communicated to many friends. In doing this, however, he may flee from himself into a turmoil of activity where he is frequently submerged.

A rightward slant together with rounded and graceful letters indicates initiative, an enterprising mind, sociability, and an expansive character with an interest in progress. Very large letters with a rightward and rounded slant betray and restrained impulse in the writer, and an impatient and unconcentrated nature. While this handwriting shows strong and passionate feelings, it may also indicate an inconsiderate and thoughtless character as in Sample 6.

Sample 8. The leftward slant symbolizes a reserve and a fear for the future which we frequently see in adolescents and children. In the adult we recognize this as an expression of a reserved attitude, bordering on the attitude of self-defense which follows disappointment and misfortune. When these writing habits are added to special characteristics of falsehood, we recognize them as a clue to dissimulation and evasion. This will be elaborated in a special chapter. When an educated person writes a childish hand,

15

he displays arrested development and a strong tendency to cling to familiar surroundings.

Sample 1. Vertical writing shows reserve, self-command, and a lack of spontaneity. This writer usually is a person with a highly critical nature, the mind rules the emotions.

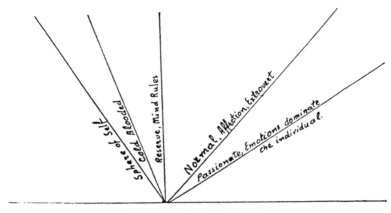

TEMPO OR SPEED

In order to ascertain speed in writing we must see whether the strokes are smoothly and securely executed. In most cases the *i*-dots and periods are assuming the form of commas or little strokes. There is an increased tendency to the right, increasing left-ward margins, short and precise initial strokes, and prolonged, lively finishing strokes. It is important to notice that there is rarely a change of slant or direction in speedy writings.

Rapidity means activity; an active mind always writes fast. Quick, large, and well-connected writing with right-ward slant and the 'i' dotted ahead, together with large left margins, reveal a character open to development and progress, as well as emotional expansiveness. S. 9.

Slow, leftward and narrow script with exactly dotted 'i's betray the hesitation of a writer who procrastinates. Speed in writing discloses an alert, lively and impulsive character, endowed with quick thought and initiative. We have to distinguish between the quick and the hasty writer,

16

for the latter is oftimes restless and unstable of character. Hastiness, together with irregular writing, discloses a lack of control.

Quick writing with a rightward slant reveals the extrovert, one who enjoys meeting people and finds his satisfaction outside of himself. *Sample 9.*

Inpulsive people, often unable to keep their thoughts on one subject without great difficulty, write a hasty hand.

He who writes slowly is also slow in his actions and reactions, and is cautious and prudent, pondering much before he acts. The introvert or the introspective person often writes a slow hand. The introvert is drawn more to his inner world, likes to be alone, and is involved in his own thoughts.

S. 2. Slow and uniform writing belongs with passive, phlegmatic and indolent natures. A very slow and dilatory hand is characteristic of melancholy, and slow, rigid, regular writing is almost always a symbol of deceit.

Pressure, slant, regularity and speed therefore indicate the writer's innate constitution and temperament. We learn from the forms, the loops and flourishes whether the writer has used his innate qualities and predispositions, affirming his capacities, or whether he has wasted them. The writer's environment is also reflected here, as well as his attitude and adaptability towards the demands of life.

CHAPTER TWO

THREE ZONES

Handwriting is divided into three zones: upper, middle and lower. Small letters such as *i,n,m,* represent the middle zone; letters containing upper length, such as *d, l, h,* form part of both middle and upper zone; letters containing lower length, such as *g,y,* form part of both middle and lower zone.

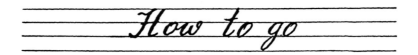

The lower zone uncovers the material and physical life, sensuality, and the world of the writer's dreams, and his subconscious life.

Middle zone expresses the conscious, unimaginative and daily life. The writer's practical intelligence, and his adaptability are discovered in the formation of the small letters.

The upper zone discloses the writer's intellectual and spiritual life, and his imaginative power and creative ideas.

Preponderance of the lower zone:

Sample 10. The loops are large and emphasized in the writing of those individuals who are physically active and who feel an affinity towards the earth and its practical needs. The farmer, hunter, and manual worker, people who are interested in material things, merchants, industrialists, and especially those who are dominated by greed, emphasize the lower zone. Sensualists, using heavy pressure, make long descending strokes with large fat loops.

S. 1.   Preponderance of the middle zone reveals practical people who are interested in their daily life, and who adapt themselves to reality.   The writer's personal interests appear in involved traits and leftward flourishes. These writers are generally narrow-minded and attach too much significance to their unimportant worries.

S. 11.   In a preponderance of the upper zone, we find the upper strokes conspicuous, as, for instance, in the writing of intellectuals, artists, scientists, and religious and idealistic persons.   In the script of the latter the *i*-dots are high and the whole writing ascends to the higher sphere. A good adjustment of the writing and plasticity, and individuality in the shaping of the letters reflect the genius and exalted person, as well as the dreamer and adventurer. We find in the futile flourishes of the upper zone the unbalanced and delirious fantasies of the insane, and all their exaggerated enthusiasms.

CONNECTIONS

From the manner in which small letters are shaped and connected with each other, we can see how the writer adapts himself to his environment and the circumstances of his life.   His affections, or his indifference, his inhibitions or emotions are reflected here.   While small letters may be shaped after the school model, they still follow the four different angles: garlands, angularity, arcades and thread or spider-like.   The genius and the highly developed intellectual, and all independent minds, create an individual style of writing.

GARLANDS

Sample 1.   This generally uncovers the good-hearted nature of an easily approachable person, who is friendly and sociable, with an adaptability to new conditions of life.

Large and rounded style with light pressure indicate an unstable and easily influenced writer who acts upon all impulses and emotions. He is extremely volatile and easily shaken by his impulses and moods.   Such a writer lacks will-power and often loses himself in a superficial life.

An excessively rounded style with a rightward slant indicates an emotional and altruistic person, one who is understanding and in sympathy with human nature. Demonstratively maternal women write a rounded style with heavy pressure. We find the garland connections in handwritings of social and accessible natures and also in those business men of practical intelligence who have dealings with different types of people. Impressionable individuals, artists, and psychologists often write garlands.

ANGULARITY   .

Sample 12.   This style of writing is typical of self-contained and reserved characters who are prudent and discreet.   They are neither pliable nor easily influenced, and although they adapt themselves to the necessities of circumstances, their feelings and real natures remain concealed.

Angularity reveals the obstinate character who tends to impose upon others.   It also indicates an active, energetic, and persistent nature which does not swerve from its feelings and principles.   In addition to these those people who rebel against customs, manners, and social laws write at times angular letters.

ARCADES

Sample 8.   This expresses a lack of spontaneity, and generally appears in the narrow writing of an inhibited person.   We find it in people who attach much importance to conventionality and formality.   We also see it in the handwritings of those individuals who live in an environment full of misunderstanding.   The arcade is almost always a characteristic of some kind of artificiality.

On the other hand, the arcade which has a unique special individual shaping of the letters reveals a creative instinct, the wish to build.   It often characterizes an artistic sense and is reflected in the handwritings of inventors, architects and engineers, as well as in those of the genius. S. 18.

Max Pulver discovers this angle in the writings of children and adolescents who were too severely educated, and who cannot, as a result, adapt themselves to the authority of a rigid environment. Arcades and angularity are present in the writings of retarded children, and in those of criminals.

Sample 13.   Regular writing coupled with angularity and heavy pressure, discloses the man of fact who is attached to his duties, whose nature is able to struggle with and overcome obstacles and hardships. We also find this in stubborn nad inflexible characters. Angularity with light pressure and leftward slant, however, discloses the timid and inhibited character. Such writers suffer quietly, keeping themselves isolated, and safe from approach.

In considering the narrow angle we generally find that it evinces prudence and reserve. Regularity coupled with narrowness is a sign of extreme self-control and a capacity for work and endurance, and characterizes a writer who will waste neither emotions nor money.

Inhibition, hypochondria, timidity, and fear of life and future are also reflected in narrowness.

If the initials are narrow, it means timidity based on inferiority complex and a sense of insufficiency. We find it in restrained characters who cannot easily make friends.

Sample 14.   The sharp and angular style with leftward and inharmonious letters show the egotist as well as the sadist.

The mixed angle (alternately garlands, angularity and arcades) indicates an adaption to various circumstances; an individual who is not always balanced in his actions and reactions.

Sample 15.   The thread or spider like angle, is found in the irregularity of the basic line which reflects the writer's nervous impressionability and emotionability. Those who write this angle react quickly to various stimuli of the external and internal worlds; they are impressionable and compliant, and know how to adapt themselves to the different conditions of life. The writer is unstable, nevertheless, and his moods are inconsistent. He will be easily interested, and attracted by, new people and events. Versatile, refined,

21

and intellectual writers with alert thoughts, unstable wills, and unbalanced emotions, write with the threadlike angle.

This style of writing is used by the psychologist who comprehends and scents with an intuitive mind, as well as the writer with weak and evasive tendencies.

The slant or angle expresses the emotional life of the writer—his power to love. The rightward angle generally shows affection; the vertical is ruled by the mind; and the leftward implies a cold-blooded and indifferent nature. When the angle slants both ways it reflects a dual nature. Pressure indicates the writer's innate constitution, his energy and physical resistance, and also the presence of diseases and organic disturbances. Pressure expresses the writer's sensuality and emotions as well as his mental strength and vitality.

The intellectual writer avoids futile strokes and often does not use connecting strokes. He displays simplicity in style and does not care to waste time or effort on extravagances of movement, or in material ways.

On the negative side, the disconnected writing with narrow and arcade letters, accompanied by a leftward slant, reveals a fear of life, and the writer does not dare face responsibilities. This person retreats from society.

However, the avaricious person who writes with a disconnected script always maintains a firm structure in his writing. He still operates on the constructive side but remains the solitary person, in spite of fame and money gained by his life.

When the structure of the writing is disssolved, rather than disconnected, it reveals acute negative qualities. Samples of this type will be shown in a later chapter.

DEFINITIONS OF GRAPHOLOGICAL TERMS

Connections: Strokes connecting the letters of a word.
Disconnections: Lapses of strokes connecting the letters of a word.
Garland: A gracious oval stroke as in a garland.

Arcade: An arched stroke resembling the architectural arcade.

Angularity: A stroke or letter with a sharp angle.

Threadlike: An almost invisible connecting stroke, terminating into nothingness.

The four graphological terms for connecting strokes are: garlands, arcades, angularity, and threadlike. These terms are also applied to the letters, *u, v, w, m,* and *n,* which often resemble strokes rather than letters.

A writing in which each word is written with one continuous stroke, each letter joined to the succeeding one is considered connected writing. This implies that the writer has logical reasoning powers. The arcade, as in *Sample* 8 is like the architectural arcade.

When we speak of a large degree of connections, we mean that the larger words are written in one movement; a mediocre degree comprises a group of words containing four or five letters; a slight degree means, everything less than that.

An interruption made in the connecting stroke by an '*i*' dot or a '*t*' crossing, as in *Sample* 9, is not considered a disconnection.

We assume that a large degree of connection must obviously signify the adaptability of a person, particularly if there is a rightward slant and a steady upward direction of the basic line.

Next there is the theoretical adaptability which may be the vertical writing or either the rightward or leftward slant. This means that the strict connecting strokes are made by a logical person or a scientist who dominates the connections in his writing.

Then we have the moral adaptability of a person who overbridges all his natural impulses as shown in strict connections of all letters even in the longest words.

If the writing persists in consistent connections without a gap between any letters and has no negative traits in the whole scheme, we can rightfully assume that the writer takes a practical and moral attitude.

However, we cannot make a virtue only of consistent regularity of the connecting stroke. The reason for this will be explained in a later chapter.

THE REASON FOR DISCONNECTIONS

When the letters in a word are separated (without the connecting stroke) we find an expression of diplomacy, an ability to mix socially and the talent to sense things intuitively. Many inventors and those who possess independence of thought and action write with a variety of disconnections. This gap in the connecting stroke is analogous to taking a breath, the pause that refreshes and permits inspiration to come through and into our consciousness. Sample 16 is a good example of an intuitive and independent thinker.

In some writings with disconnected letters which can be connected easily, we discover that the person is absorbed in his work but is perfectly able to manage his practical life. Sample 17 is an example of such a writing.

Sometimes we find a combination of disconnected letters which indicate that the person scents the situation before he has decided to act upon it.

CHAPTER THREE

SMALL LETTERS

The breadth of writing is measured according to the proportion of the letter. For instance in the letter '*n*' we compare the distance between the two downstrokes with the length of the downstrokes themselves. If the downstrokes are longer than the distance, between them, we have narrow writing; if they are shorter, it is considered wide writing. S. 12 narrow, S. 13 wide.

THE PERSONAL PRONOUN OF THE FIRST PERSON SINGULAR

In the Anglo-Saxon language the graphologist must attach a great deal of importance to the capital '*I*' when it is used as the personal pronoun. English is the only language in which the personal pronoun of the first person singular, '*I*' is written with a capital.

The capital '*I*' is an important factor for the interpretation of American handwriting. We are a people who know, "I can be what I want to be." This subconcious realization of our personal freedom necessarily injects dramatic reality into the letter. In the capital '*I*', its simplicity refllects modesty and degrees of refinement; exaggerated loops and artificial flourishes express ostentation. The aspects of the personal pronoun capital '*I*' are transferred from the character to the personality, whereas, in the other capital the aspects are used to impress. The capital '*I*' when used as the personal pronoun is a dominating indicator of what the writer thinks of himself, and the other capitals are indicators of what the writer wants the world to think of him or what he longs to be.

SOMETHING ABOUT THE CAPITALS

The capital letter is impressive. We attach a dignity to it by its size and design; it is formed purposely to impress. It makes its bow at the beginning of a sentence, it impresses you harmoniously or otherwise. It is the personal expression of what the man wants the world to think of him. In the modest capital the personal motive can be interpreted as a constructive one.

When we find a highly embellished capital, we realize that the writer longs to be someone he fears he cannot be. This actual limitation or his belief as to his own inferiority are immediately revealed. The would-be gentleman is impelled to make flourishes to impress the public. He has unsatisfied aspirations and imitates the elaborate capitals found in the scripts of those who have caught the attention of the public through their conquest or through their belief of divine inheritance.

In exaggerated cases of the inflated ego the capital letter is enlarged and ornamented with flourishes in a hysterical attempt to attract attention. The inflated capital is the would-be gentleman's persona. It is the mask over a weak character or poor personality. The well formed capital letter, in size and shape is also the persona of the writer, but of a gentleman who is genuine in his unmasked moments as well as when he is in social contact with the world. The undersized capital indicates a lack of faith in self, and ones own ability.

In general the capital letter can be judged as a constructive feature if it conforms to a moderate size with graceful formations.

Opposite conclusions can be made if there is undue exaggeration and awkward formations.

Originality in the capital letters is often found in the writing of creative artists.

Ornate capitals cannot be criticized in the Latin races; their expression is more lively than the Anglo-Saxon.

The Englishman's code of behavior is restrained; he modifies his capitals. When exaggeration of capitals occurs in the handwriting of an English person, a parallel trait can be found in the character or personality.

In the American script we cannot be too severe in our

judgment of moderately exaggerated capitals used by the aggressive business man.

The initial and final strokes also have their value and it is justifiable to note their presence, especially if they repeat themselves throughout the writing. When there is a repetition of conspicuous or conventional strokes, the graphologist should try to uncover the reason. Marked repetition of initial and final strokes usually is a sign of some deep rooted cause or oddity, the source is usually negative and the cause should be uncovered and corrected.

STUDY IN NUMBERS

Let us deal here with numbers as a symbol of material values. As such they are expressive of the emotional and impulsive attitude of the writer towards material values. Very often a talent or a lack of talent, for monetary matters shows itself much more clearly in the shaping of numbers than in that of words.

Sample 19 shows a writer with a characteristic talent for monetary matters. The numbers are smoothly written, and display certainty of aim, nimbleness and experience. The essential nature of the shape is grasped and presented in a precise, clear, and simple manner, the tempo is quick, the legibility good. We deduce from this that the writer is a reliable and quick reckoner, talented for monetary matters, and that his attitude towards material value is reasonable.

In contrast to this writer we find a group of people who for some reason or other are ungifted for monetary matters. An illustration of this type will be found in S. 20, which is characterized by clumsily and awkwardly drawn numbers in an otherwise fluent handwriting. This writer, generally intelligent and gifted, is reduced to helplessness the moment he has to tackle numbers. He is unable to calculate without effort and makes mistakes in the most simple problem. It is his number-writing which shows that he is a poor reckoner, and that he has no understanding of the concept of numbers.

Sometimes, however, the desire to accumulate earthly treasures is shown in numbers. Sample 21 gives evidence of extremely full numbers, which are very skillfully executed, written with libidinous pressure, and they are extremely large. The nimbleness of execution indicates a good reckoner, the fullness, the pressure, and the size of numbers together with very large and inflated lower loops betray the extremely strong libido, the powerful wish-fantasy and the insatiable greed which characterizes the number conception of the writer. He is an excessive spender and will not stop at criminal acts in order to satisfy his sensuous aspirations.

From these examples we may infer that number writing is expressive of the talent as well as of the behavior of the writer in monetary and financial matters, and that in certain cases numbers can be psychologically more revealing than words.

STUDY IN MARGINS

When the margin on both sides is in proportion to the width of paper and size in writing we may conclude that the writer has a proper regard for neatness and order, accompanied by good taste, sense of proportion and balance and poise. (S. 1.)

S. 6. If the margins on both sides are too narrow, or even missing entirely, an evident lack of good taste is manifested. There also will be a confirmation of thrift, or even of miserliness, according to the evidence of the crowded line and other ruling characteristics revealed in the script itself.

Sometimes the margin on the left side is wide in proportion to the width of paper and size of writing. This generally indicates an instinct or desire for originality. S. 64.

When the margin on the right hand side is absurdly wide in proportion to width of paper and size of writing, it is conclusive that the writer is either wasteful and extravagant, or has grandiose ideas with much immoderation in gratifying them. Such writers, if impulsiveness is evident, will blindly go to extremes. There are exceptions to this rule, of course, but they will be readily recognized. S. 24.

28

Of relatively little significance is the upper margin, if it is extremely large, it almost always is a sign of great respect to the addressee. This form of margin is mostly used in conventional letters.

The lower margin may be missing entirely and the writing may be crowded to the bottom of the page, leaving no room for a lower margin. This is not regarded as a negative trait because of necessity.

If however, the lower margin corresponds with the good taste of the side and upper margin, we recognize the culture of the writer.

In considering margins it will be well to observe carefully the address of the e n v e l o p e. Addresses which are in harmony with the writing will generally be found to confirm signs of proportion and good taste, culture, breeding and artistic sense, and will be found to coincide with the margin in the writing itself. Envelope addresses are very important; first they carry several capital letters revealing important truths, and secondly they express the writer's attitude toward public and social life.

The purpose of an address is that the letter should reach the addressee without any difficulty. This purpose is only served by a high degree of legibility and clearness of the writing and its arrangement. Accordingly many people do write more legibly on the envelope than in the letter itself. (*Sample* 19).

A case of illegibility on an envelope signifies psychological difficulties in a writer to observe conventional considerations. It indicates a special disturbance in regard to adaptation which is characteristic of people who are difficult in personal as well as social intercourse. S. 110.

SIGNATURE

The signature is the writer's social ego. From it we can infer his attitude towards social and public life, and how he displays his personality.

Psychologically revealing are divergencies between signature and writing, regarding the size of handwriting,

29

which may be large or small in comparison with the body of the writing.

In the case of a larger signature with otherwise smaller handwriting as in Sample 69, the writer wants to over-emphasize himself; perhaps a certain lack of self-reliance prompts him to be impressive. One fact seems sure, the higher the degree of individuation in a person the less he is prone to make himself dependent upon public opinion, a dependence which finds expression n the divergence of size between the signature and the writing, or in some kind of flourish. Underscoring as in Sample 11, comes under this heading also.

In dealing with this feature we have to take into consideration at which period a document was written, (*signature of Goethe*) as well as national differences. Writers of Latin nationalities often adorn their signatures to a degree of complete illegibility.

The signature to a certain extent is a mere facade, especially in handwritings of people who appear in public. It is adorned with many flourishes, or underscored, this giving great importance to the writer's mental attitude concernig himself. S. 49. The signature can be modelled in different ways in some cases it impresses as a pose in a theatrical act; in others, however, it pictures the writer's self-conscious and timid personality.

CHAPTER FOUR

THE TEMPERAMENTS

Modern psychology has detached itself from the antique definition of temperamental types, but we must admit that science has not totally freed itself from the belief that there are four temperaments- a concept which dates back to the remote age when men first began to investigate psychic life. The division of the temperaments into sanguine, choleric, melancholic and phlegmatic belongs to Hippocrates. From ancient Greece it found its way to Rome, and today remains an honorable relic in the midst of our present psychology.

The sanguine type governs those individuals who evince pleasure in life, who do not take things too seriously, and who attempt to see the most pleasant and beautiful side of every event. When the occasion demands, they are sad, but temperately so, without breaking down. On the other hand, they derive pleasure from happy events without a loss of perspective in their rejoicing. They are generally positive, and healthy in mind and body.

Sample 22. A sanguine temperament, an impressionable type:

The quick features written with even pressure, and the long low loops show that this young woman possesses an intelligent and active nature, filled with the emotion and affection of the sensual type. She is very impressionable, and reacts to every stimulus and impression of the external world. The large and rightward angle betrays the writer's interest in life and the future. The unequalness of the size and height of the letters discloses, however, her lack of control and perseverance. An instability of interests, and even of purpose, prevents her from following a consistent pattern of activity. She possesses artistic and intellectual abilities, and shows, through the width and largeness of her letters, an enthusiastic and adventurous mind.

This woman occasionally dedicates herself with fervor to studies and ambitious aims of which she soon wearies. Though she is positive and able, it is difficult for her to remain for long in the same environment, and engaged in the same work. While at the beginning everything seems attractive and rich in prospects, it becomes annoying as time goes on. Not knowing how to discipline herself and her moods, she may run the risk of wasting her life, in spite of her manifold abilities.

The melancholic temperament, and sensitive type:

This type is the consistently hesitating neurotic who has no confidence in his ability to overcome difficulties, or to succeed in anything. Rather than risk a new adventure, he would prefer to remain still, even in sight of his goal. If such an individual does drive himself forward, he only begins each movement with the greatest caution. Doubt plays a prominent part in his life.

This type of man thinks much more about himself than about others, and this attitude eventually excludes him from happier possibilities. Therefore he can only stare back into his past, or spend his time in fruitless introspection.

Sample 23. The handwriting of this thirty-five-year old woman mirrors her passivity and lack of initiative. She is a most talented musician, but has no success because she will not take advantage of her gifts. In comparison to her aptitude and high inelligence, her writing assumes a rather slow tempo, and shows heavy falling endings, uncovering the fatigue which inhibits her actions. This woman is easily discouraged; she needs to gain self-confidence and must learn to rely upon her great musical talent. She lives in an imaginary world and lacks the courage to bring herself back to ambition and reality.

The unequalness in the size and height of all her

letters, together with the wavering basic line, show her sensibility as well as her lack of physical resistance.

The choleric temperament and excitable type:

The choleric individual is one whose striving for power is so intense that his whole life is based upon emphatic and violent actions, for he feels that he is forced to demonstrate his power at all times. He believes that he is forced to overcome all obstacles, and does so in an aggressively straight-line approach. We find that the first intense movements of these individuals begin in their early childhood, when they lacked a realization of their power, and were forced to demonstrate it on every occasion in order to convince themselves of its existence.

Sample 24. Excitability is revealed in the sudden pressure or an occasional stroke of this rather light writing, together with angularity. The rightward slant discloses liveliness and a sociable nature. The narrow angle reveals, however, a reserved and self-contained character who displays reticence concerning his personal affairs.

The small writing of this intelligent and well-educated man shows that he is a keen observer, and that he will forget neither his own faults, nor the injuries which he has received. He is exceedingly depressed by his failures, but is not apt to display his feeling publicly. He generally conceals his suffering, but his emotions sometimes explode in the form of vehement words and actions. In his use of pointed angles, his tendency towards sarcastic criticism is revealed.

The small and angular style of writing indicates his perseverance, and the inexhaustible energy which he exerts for the realization of his projects. This man is endowed with a clear and alert intellect (well-spaced words and letters), coupled with sticktoitiveness and a great depth of passion. Since he is excessively ambitious, he completely exhausts his energies, and spends his life in a turmoil of activity, feeling ill-at-ease when he is forced into inaction.

33

The phlegmatic temperament, or the indolent type:

This type of person is, in general, a stranger to life. He gathers impressions, but cannot follow them to their appropriate conclusions. Nothing can make a great impression on him; he is barely interested in anything; he makes no friends, and in short has almost no connection with life. Of all the types, it is he, perhaps, who stands at the greatest distance from the business of living.

Sample 25. This handwriting is typical of the low impressionability and sluggishness of the phlegmatic merchant. The slow and monotonous traits indicate the writer's dulled reaction to any stimulus from the external world. Indeed, he is not easily brought out of himself. This young man exhibits a calm attitude which expresses itself in slow gestures. The regular writing reveals self - control, pertinacity and prudence. He is incapable of any passionate impulse and will never be driven by immoderate aims. When he is occupied in a position which has been provided for him by Providence, he will avoid any changes, though he utilizes all his abilities. He maintains his mental balance, and remains happy or unhappy.

In spite of what we have seen, clearly defined temperaments are seldom found. Generally one deals with admixtures of one or more types, and even then they are not fixed. Frequently we find that one temperament dissolves into another, as when a child who begins life as a choleric individual, later becomes melancholic, only to end his life as a phlegmatic. Of all types, the sanguine seems to have been least exposed to any feelings of inferiority in childhood, and as a result has been allowed to follow his own bent, and develop into maturity with a certain love for life which enables him to approach it on a surer footing. There is no individual who is phlegmatic during the entire course of his life. We must realize that his temperament is only a shell, a defense mechanism which an over-sensitive being has created for himself, a fortification which he has thrown between himself and the outer world.

34

CHAPTER FIVE

HANDWRITING OF THE CHILD

In the first years of the child's life, as in those of the animal, we are able to distinguish special characteristics. Distinct and outspoken qualities, however, are not so clearly manifested in early childhood. Basic mental and physical dispositions, on the other hand, make themselves apparent at a relatively early age.

We must differentiate between those traits which are inborn, those which have been acquired, and those influenced by environment. Education can either favor or hamper the development of the youngster. For instance, wrong guidance may spoil a good disposition, or a poor one may be corrected through intelligent training.

Children become 'problem children' because they interpret negative experience in terms of defeat. To protect them from feelings of inferiority, they should be taught that all of us can learn only through our own experience. Every child is overshadowed by the threat of a potentially warped development. This threat most often becomes a reality through the injury of his not having been taken seriously. The custom of telling children palpable lies, and especially that of subjecting them to ridicule, can be called criminal acts. One important basis for this injurious attitude has its existence in the emphasis which has been placed on ambition as a superlative virtue, which permeates the child's education. No matter where he turns, the child is confronted with the model of the individual who is greater, better and more glorious than his fellows. Children should be taught that anyone can find his own place in life.

We now realize that mothers and teachers must learn as much from their children as they teach. It requires much experience and comprehension to recognize the child's latent strength and shortcomings, and his particular gifts, and to know where to encourage and where to curb.

A child's personality is very closely allied to his handwriting, and herein lies the best opportunity to determine and correct his individuality as well as to help in improving the comprehension of those people who are responsible for his development.

After two to three years of writing in ink, the child has generally developed a certain freedom of writing, has learned how to familiarize himself with writing materials, and has attained his own style of writing. Consequently, we have now reached the point where we are able to judge the youngsters frankly.

Mothers and teachers should not try to mould the minds of their children into a uniform model of excellency; instead, they should respect the gradually developing individuality of the child. We have benefited by the mistakes of our parents and grandparents, and we must now free ourselves from their prejudices, and face things as they actually are.

The graphologist and the psychologist can help in solving these complicated problems. Our most important task is to avoid difficulties before they can take a tangible form.

Sample 26. This eleven-year-old boy shows a strong intellectual inclination which is revealed by the clear and simplified formation of his letters. Relative speed denotes his independent nature which is endowed with great potentialities. We shall notice, however, that the boy has a nervous excitability which comes to light in the change of slant and trembling strokes. He might become a problem child if he is not watched and guided carefully.

Sample 27. In the narrow angle with a leftward slant we see a very restrained and reserved character which influences the handwriting of this twelve-year-old boy. The independent formation of his letters proves him to be intelligent and able, while the firm strokes show his energy as well as his capacity for sustained effort. He will find it difficult to confide in his companious, and is even diffident

and touchy. His basic need is for the affectionate understanding of his mother, who could develop in him a more expansive
nature, and genuine cooperativeness. He is often despond-
ent and in need of encouragement. The angularity uncovers his talent for mechanics and construction,

Sample 28. The continual change of slant reveals that
the emotional life of this twelve-year-old girl fluctuates
between her mind and heart. On one occasion she is
demonstrative, on another, cold and indifferent. She is
easily discouraged, and when she is, her whole writing seems
to fall. Emphasis of the upper zone reflects her imagination
and independence of thought, but while she is clever and
intelligent, the standard of her work is unpredictable. This
girl should be trained to systematize her work, and to
develop concentration since she is easily distracted.

Sample 29. Here we see a twelve-year-old boy whose
personality has already been formed. The rightward and
regular slant shows his affectionate nature; his pliable
character is revealed by the lower loops. He has almost
developed a matter-of-fact routine in handling his writing
materials, and has acquired a definite rhythm and idividual
speed. He obviously has a harmonious life where his
parents understand and guide him with comprehension.

Sample 30. A capacity for work makes this thirteen-
year-old girl appear older than she is. She is clever, and
is conscientious in the performance of her tasks. The well-
spaced words show her clearness of ideas, and the small writing uncovers her aptitude for concentrated study. From
the crossing of the *t*'s, we learn of her obstinacy which
borders on stubbornness. (The dashes are made with
heavy pressure, contrasting with the light pressure of the
whole body of the writing). While the rounded angle
reveals her kind-hearted nature, she displays a tendency to
dominate her companions.

Sample 31. This boy of twelve has succeded, to an
amazing degree, in forming his personality and individuality.
He is very emotional, and often gives way to an unbalanced
expression of his feelings. He is lethargic in performing

37

his assignments, and sometimes his laziness is great enough to require stimulation. Manual dexterity is uncovered in his angular style. The wavy "*t*" dashes disclose the fact that his will is more pliant than powerful, and he has wit and a sense of humor. This boy should have steady guidance, and if necessary severe discipline, if he is to overcome his shortcomings, and develop his strong points.

Sample 32. The delicate pressure of this twelve-year-old girl reveals her tender and sympathetic nature. She is thoughtful and careful, and far from unintelligent. Perhaps it would be better for her if she were a little less considerate of others. From the well-spaced letters and words we can see her clear and logical way of thinking, though she is somewhat touchy and at times needs encouragement.

Sample 33. The writing of this twelve-year-old boy displays great cleverness, but also shows lack of effort in his working habits. The individual shaping of letters reveals both his alertness and his relatively independent thinking, although he has neither concentration nor a sense of order. He is flexible, emotional and affectionate. He needs strong and intelligent guidance, as well as the imposition of routine tasks. His writing shows the inattention and laziness which he must obviously overcome; while his heavy downstrokes reveal his obstinacy and cantankerousness.

Sample 34. We see a nervous irritability in the handwriting of this boy of eleven. He has a lively temperament and, for his age, possesses a highly developed mental ability. He has not yet succeeded, however, in expressing his personality, which swings backward and forward like an emotional pendulum. He is intrinsically self-conscious, and thrusts himself forward, always trying to impress his fellows. He is evasive, concealing and even distorting the truth. He shows a tendency towards diffidence, does not readily confide in others, and is unwilling to cooperate. This boy needs strict but understanding guidance, since he can be called a problem child.

From the manner, then, in which the child masters

the problem of writing and its aspects, we are able to draw certain conclusions regarding his definite faculties, in addition to providing his educators with helpful material to guide the choice of his future career.

We would be wrong, however, in assuming that every child has a potential career. Such is by no means the case, since it is safe to say that the majority of children of average ability would have equal chance in a number of different occupations, as long as they had previously received such training as would be necessary.

CHAPTER SIX

HOW WE CAN GUIDE OUR CHILDREN THROUGH HANDWRITING ANALYSIS

During the many years that I have been analyzing handwriting of young people, I have found a number of excellent character traits; however, my analyses have shown serious misuse of good traits, and abilities left to deteriorate.

One important fact is that our culture unfortunately seems permeated with the spurring on of ambition for grandeur in the mind of our youth. Too much emphasis is placed by some individuals upon those qualities which they think makes them better, greater, and more glorious than their fellow-men. Young people should be taught that any one can find his place in life when he learns how to use his abitities.

Usually young folk have great possibilities, but under a mistaken understanding, or indifference, many parents ignore t h e i r responsibilities until it is too late, or ignore them completely.

The handwriting of the youngster gives clear indication of his personality and offers an opportunity to determine and improve character traits and abilities, and also help to broaden the understanding of those who are responsible for the children's good development. Many sons and daughters have come to me, asking how to correct weaknesses and how to conquer shortcomings, and they listened eagerly to my interpretation of their writings. I discovered their good points and their weaknesses, have weighed and evaluated them, and then tried to work out the plan of living that would use the good qualities. On the other hand, mothers and fathers have come to me, saying that they did not know what to do with so-called problem children, when a study of the parent's writing indicated that the boy could not be anything but a problem child if he reflected the father's nature.

My experience in analyzing people, studying their motives, working with them in a sincere desire to help them, has convinced me that parents who have trouble at home should start having their own handwriting analyzed, and then their children's. The latter they will find amazingly encouraging, and their own specimen may give enough reason for immediate and detailed alibis.

Most of the problem girls and boys whose handwriting specimens have been submitted to me by worried parents show that they are not bad but misguided. On the other hand brilliant children, who have attracted great public favor have not been merely talented, but they have had the benefit of training from parents who knew that the child represented a responsibility.

Sample 35. This girl of almost seventeen wants to know her special talents. The rightward slant uncovers her strong emotions, and the pasty pressure mirrors her impressionable nature. The open loops of the *"d"* and *"t"* reflect her sensitiveness. The height of the stems show her readiness to feel imposed upon and to resent that imposition. Such a writer is always prone to believe that others are planning to take advantage. This girl pretends to be an artist, actress or writer, and she resents having grown up in poverty which impeded her development and growth. In fact she has no special talent and would hardly become an artist even with the best instruction, She has only an average intelligence, has as yet not succeded in forming her personality and individuality.

She begins words with an inflexible stroke starting at the middle zone disclosing a character which is on the defensive most of the time, if not all the time. In this case a loving and understanding mother could help her to find her way, but she is neglected and lacks love and affection.

Sample 36. This is an interesting specimen of a girl of thirteen. The individual letter formations bespeak her independence of thought and her originality. The rhythmical adjustment of the whole writing mirrors her sense of musical rhythm and artistic ability. She is a dancer and was already on the stage in early childhood.

True enough Phyllis has talent, and it was fortunate that the talent was outstanding enough to be cultivated.

However, your boy or your girl may have talent, and unless that ability is discovered, may drift along aimlessly for years. Handwriting is a clear and true picture of all abilities, and through uncovering these talents we can point out the direction in which the youngster's talent leads him.

The following specimens 37, 38, 39, 40, will tell us a story of a girl who through favorable development, understanding guidance plus talent succeeded in forming her little personality already at the age of eight. We notice in sample 37 that the letter formations deviate from the school-model reflecting her desire of independence in thought and action. The good adjustment of the whole writing reveals her artistic ability and sense of musical rhythm. The good spacing discloses her clear mind and sense of order, while her emotional nature is expressed in the garlands and rightward angle.

Sample 38 shows her at the age of twelve where she has arrived at a high point of mental development. The heavy '*t*' bars show that she wants her own way at all costs and begins to rebel against the authority of her parents. Conspicuous are the high finals bespeaking her ideals and a high standard of integrity. The decided downstrokes of the "*y*" together with the triangle of some lower loops discover

41

her perseverance and energy in accomplishing tasks. Some "o"s and "a"s are open and some are closed showing her frankness on the one hand and on the other, that she is capable of keeping to herself things that should not be told.

Original letter formations plus garlands reveal that she is emotionally expressive and generous without extravagance. Her already developed talent for music expresses itself in the warm pressure and rhythmical spacing of words.

Sample 39 pictures this girl at fourteen. The style of writing is now narrow and the vowels are almost firmly closed. She seems somewhat emotionally upset and became extremely sensitive and reserved. She is involved in her own problems and not inclined toward social contact and companionship. Although she is faithful to her old friends she will not be ready to make new friendships. Her hard struggle in finding her way is shown in the so-called wiry strokes. She feels that her parents do not understand her anymore and that she has to depend on her own decisions. The heavy pressure reflects her ardent ambition to be the best in school and the narrow angle her utmost economy for time.

Sample 40 shows that the now eighteen-year-old-girl has perfectly succeeded in forming her personality and individuality. In comparison to the previous sample we notice here change in slant and speed uncovering her pronounced musical talent. The pressure remained heavy and the basic line became steady revealing the moral strength to make the most of her gift. She possesses good judgment and criticism, expressed in the vertical angle, and the deeply garlanded connections reveal her depth of feeling.

We can predict to a certain extent that this writer will make a success of her life, and that she will not bow down to the opinion of others but will go her own individual way.

Sample 41 and 42 belong to boys of twelve and ten who are brothers. Unfortunately they live in an environment most unfavorable for their dispositions. Their mother is physically weak and shiftless, and the father a poor provider.

S. 41. The narrow angle coupled with closed and involved vowels in the script of the older boy, reveal his secretive and suspicious nature. The heavy "*t*" bars disclose temper and violence. However, he possesses sufficient self-control to appear different from what he really is. He displays a certain amount of ambition and intelligence plus general abilities which should enable him to play his part in life, provided he had the right guidance. He is a coward, however, and shows some criminal tendencies. He lies, is always on the defensive and tries to conceal his thoughts. Since he has not the courage to commit theft himself, he influences his smaller brother who is only a tool in his hands, to steal for him.

Sample 42 shows the younger boy, whose unsteady writing betrays his weakness of character. The very slow script with the continual change in slant uncover laziness and utmost lack of ambition and will-power.

We can predict that both boys may become criminals, however, an understanding guidance could save them and make them both useful to the community.

CHAPTER SEVEN

DEVELOPMENT OF PERSONALITY

Disraeli wrote in *Vivian Grey*, "Man is not the creature of circumstances, circumstances are the creatures of man". A deep understanding of life teaches us that we are not the victims of environment, but that, on the contrary, outward conditions are the manifestations of our positive or negative thoughts. Indubitably, we are able to control our thoughts and through them our conditions, provided that we are emotionally balanced.

It often happens that a man who has always been successful in life is suddenly subject to melancholy, for no tangible reason. During his lifelong drive for success, he has been selfishly wrapped up in his own affairs. At the peak of his maturity, however, he begins to observe the emptiness of his personal life, and accordingly becomes discontented. He has remained immature since he has not succeded in forming his personality. Oftimes a mental collapse is inevitable: he suffers like a child, abandoned in the dark, and unable to find the way out.

Only a few people have grown to an individual maturity without meeting any obstacles which would arrest their development. We often find persons at a blockade in the path of their evolution, whose resulting growth is extremely retarded. They are generally unquiet and discontented, and always complain of their bad luck. Sooner or later, however, nature demands its fulfillment. and then a physic- al disease often results as the consequence of this mental dissatisfaction.

We recognize three different stages of evolution: 1) the forming of character, 2) the development of personality, and 3) the forming of individuality. In the first stage, primary knowledge is acquired, and the character begins to form. The child learns how to distinguish between good and bad, sorrow and joy, pleasant and unpleasant feelings. With the help of wise guidance, the child accepts the dis- cipline of his tasks, and learns how to adapt himself to his environment; affections, social feelings and the ability to cooperate now develop. When years of education are finished, the period of a freer evolution begins. The adult of good innate disposition, who has grown up in a favorable environment, will make an easy choice of career. He is full of prospects, and is eager to follow his own path, leaving the accustomed surrounding of childhood's ties. Now he must prove whether his character is weak or strong.

This specimen of *Sample* 43 clearly shows the above- mentioned arrested development. It is the handwriting of a fifty-year-old woman. The childish traits with change of slant reveal that the thoughts of this writer are permanently attached to her childhood and adolescence. Her recollect- ions have become treasures which impede her progress, success, and above all adaptability to a new environment. She is obstinate in her refusal to take any interest in the

44

new conditions of life, since she has always depended, both physically and mentally, on the customs of her parents' home. We see sudden vertical letters in the rightward angle which denote such resistence. While her general disposition tends to optimism, she is, however, easily shaken by untoward events. Since she is always emphasizing the unfavorable occurrences in life, she is almost definitely predestined to be unhappy. She is fearful of any change, and especially of an unknown future.

Sample 44. This is the handwriting of a young woman of twenty-five. We see her arrested development in her fairly large writing with narrow angle which slants to the left. This shows her to be a timid person who is afraid of the future and its uncertainties. She has a firm character, but cannot easily express herself, and shuts herself away from social contacts. Though she has a sensual nature (heavy pressure and long lower loops) and needs affection, she avoids young men, and represses her natural instincts and emotions. Since she can never make up her mind, she lacks the incentive to leave her familiar surroundings and begin a life of her own. Her inferiority complex and fearfulness impede what could be an active life, and drain her physical resistance.

This is the age when the formation of personality and individuality should normally have begun; when exaggerated affections and a childish adherence to an accustomed environment should be left behind. Most young men and women lack the courage to act upon their instincts, though an inner will to free themselves generally exists. This will often manifest itself in a rebellion against traditions. There are people, however, who while continuing in an opposition to the demands of their environment, until old age, are so weak and indeterminate that they lose their opportunities and connections.

Sample 45. We notice an exaggerated attitude of rebellion and self-defense in the handwriting of this woman of thirty; an attitude which we occasionally find during the periods of puberty and adolescence. She is a very gifted and willful person who has not yet succeded in maturing her personality and individuality. She always places the responsibility for her own shortcomings on her environment rather than herself. The constant change of slant shows, on the one hand, her rebellion, and on the other, her inability to stand on her own feet.

This magnified attitude of rebellion which is expressed in violent movements of the pen, seems like the cry: "Let me go my own way. Let me be independent." The looped and unequal handwriting reveals her vacillating nature and weak will. Her realization of her own weakness drives her to repeated rebellions. She often displays temper and is, at times, made insupportable by her lack of control.

Generally such periods of protest should disappear with the emergence of the adult personality which heralds the reality of life. The creation of a career brings an enlargement of interests, and leaves no room for childish insubordinations.

Sample 46. The too wide and violent pen movements have disappeared in the handwriting of this twenty-six-year-old man. We notice through the simplified letters, which run rapidly to the right, that the writer has become quiet and objective, looking forward to a career and its possibilities. An indication of boyish feelings is still visible in an awkward curling of the capital *e's,* but, the writing, in its entirety, is formed with character. He knows how to manage his own life, and already wishes to marry and settle down.

At maturity, individuals should arrive at a certain freedom of action, when their selfish wishes should disappear and larger social problems arise to enrich their interests, and prevent the following years from becoming empty and distasteful.

Sample 47. We notice a case of arrested development which is manisfested in the script of this fifty-year-old woman through her childish signs and backward strokes. This writer cherishes dreams of youth and illusion, instead of resigning herself to her duties as wife and mother, and finding her satisfaction in an affection for, and care of her family. Her husband and children suffer at the hands of her egotistic and schizophrenic dreams. Her false romanticism is uncovered by the capital *"M"*s and the sudden leftward slant of her cramped writing.

Sample 48. In the writing of this fifty-year-old-man, we see the consistently indefined formation of his letters, as well as an unnaturally restricted style of writing in general, which reveal his selfish drive to make life unpleasant for all his fellow beings. He has a continuous feeling of lassitude, and is often in a depressed and nervous state of mind. He repeatedly seeks a return to health in different resorts, but naturally cannot find a cure there for his malingering, since his general health is satisfactory. Psychic infantilism is the reason for his hypochondria, since this man, though physically mature, has remained undeveloped and childish, The diminutive proportions of his letters clearly reveal his self-centered ideas, and we notice selfish avidity and vain ambition expressed in his consciously minimized lower loops. This diminution is obviously premeditated since the initials of his signature—a symbol of his self-importance—bring to light the real estimation of himself in an inconsistent freedom of the letters.

Sample 49. From the individual shaping of letters we discern the writer's culture, talents and intuition. Understanding and altruism are revealed in the rightward slant and heavy pressure of the script. This writer is not concerned with his problems alone, but has learned to forget himself in a greater fulfillment of life, as well as helping those who call upon him for assistance. Because of this, he has reached a harmonious state of mind based on a well-grounded philosophy. This is the handwriting of the pianist Carl Friedberg.

The seed of positive evolution can be planted through the child's recognition of the existence of the external world, and his beginning to understand the first rules and laws of life. Next, the pleasure of accomplishing his tasks, the development of affectionate and social feelings advance this evolution. The adolescent tries to comprehend life and to free himself from the constraining ties of childhood— he wants to find his own way, and follow wherever it leads him. This is the natural time for the formation of the personality, the realization of the evolution. The young man learns how to master his life. Now his own fate is not the only center of his interests, and the selfish wishes of his childhood change into a wider universal horizon, opening into an altruistic concept of thought. The importance of his own personality gradually fades into a harmony which means mental balance and social adjustment.

When he is in deep communion with nature and the universe, man comprehends the eternal laws of creation to which we are all subject. He feels himself to be a part of the cosmos, and knows that he is a responsible member of his community, that he must contribute to the good of the whole through his strength of character and true faith in God.

CHAPTER EIGHT

PARTNERSHIP IN BUSINESS AND MARRIAGE

It very often happens that two rival employees in important positions, or two business partners, although successful as individuals, are unable to collaborate. In such a case graphological analysis can either ensure one partner's greater appreciation of the personality of the other, or show that both are so different in their personalities and opinions that they must establish a new basis of collaboration.

If we ask ourselves in connection with S. 50 and 51 why any partnership seems to be out of the question, we shall arrive at the following facts: Both men are capable and efficient in their own way, but the difference between their personalities is too great to be overbridged. The writer of S. 50 is correct to the point of being pedantic, prefers a quiet steady business procedure which follows a tradition of small safe profits.

The writer of S. 51 is much more versatile, enterprising, daring and speculative, is inclined to affect modern business methods and transacts his business on a large scale. He has little feeling for tradition, and in the long run prefers considerable profits at great risks to small and safely calculated gains.

Their characters are of such difference, and their business methods are so much opposed to each other, that they will be always at cross purposes. In such a case as this the graphological analysis will enable the two partners to decide whether or not their personalities and views are so divergent that they cannot possibly be reconciled, and if they are how to effect a friendly separation.

To take a different type of partnership: if two people are planning to be married it is usually advisable to consult the graphologist, although we must admit that in such an event either case should receive the most delicate and responsible handling on the part of the graphologist. It is not the object of such an analysis to bring two people together or to separate them, but simply to prepare them for the greatest understanding and appreciation of each other that they can possibly feel.

Here we will show a following typical example - the handwritings of two people who are engaged.

Sample 52 shows the handwriting of the man who is skilled and well trained although somewhat indulgent and very emotional. The round and connected traits discover his most adaptable and pliable nature. He is not quick in his decisions, easily influenced, depending partly on the opinions of others. S. 53 shows the writing of a girl who is very self-assured and possesive; the vertical writing and the heavy down strokes coupled with angular lower loops mirror her obstinacy and desire to have her own way at all costs. Whether this will be a good match is more than doubtful, because their handwritings indicate that the girl will dominate the man and further impede his basically weak nature, retarding any possible development by making him self-conscious and consequently unhappy.

In this case the graphologist can advise these two young people to reconsider very seriously before they come to any decision.

Not only when marriage is being contemplated, but also during the course of married life a serious conflict or important situation may arise which would make it expedient to consult a graphologist.

CHAPTER NINE

MAN WITH PRACTICAL INTELLIGENCE

The farmer, the hunter, the fisherman and the gardener are all attached to the earth, and therefore to the material world. They must use their practical intelligence in order to be able to live by their work. Their activity is concentrated on their functional and daily life, therefore their handwriting mirrors their realization of their physical needs.

Sample 54. Here we see the writing of a farmer, whose heavy hand is awkward and unused to forming the letters. From the rightward angle, however, we discover his honesty and sincerity.

The handwritings of farmers and other manual laborers are not very different from those of children. While heavy pressure reveals a powerful man, the childish shape of the letters reflects their primitive and untrained minds. The preponderance of the lower zone characterizes the man who is dominated by the earth's materiality.

Sample 55. This writing is that of a thirty-year-old female cook. A short glance suffices to reveal her simple thoughts, and sound common sense. Her occasionally ornate letters are a result of the old fashioned style of writing which she was taught. The relatively well-spaced letters and their rightward angle show her orderly practicality, and her adaptation to the demands of daily life.

Sample 56. From the writing of this carpenter we see the traits of a skilled worker, his methodical exactness. He is already seventy years old. Some of the unusual characteristics of his writing are due to his learning a foreign method of penmanship.

Sample 57. This is the writing of a woman who earns her living as a gardener. Her good taste is revealed by the adjustment of her script as a whole, and her sense of duty by the clearness of her letters. The long lower loops show her practical sense.

Sample 58. In this writing we see the manual dexterity of a mechanic who executes his work with exactness and punctuality. The very long lower loops mirror the practical and materialistic man. We also see his sense of organization in the parallel slant of all his up and down strokes.

Sample 59. This tradesman's writing uncovers his materialistic and practical sense. The letters are nicely shaped, which reflect his ability to handle his customers shrewdly. We again see the long lower loops and predominance of the lower zone which characterize this type of person.

Sample 60. This is the script of a salesman. Though the emphasis of the lower zone shows his materialistic sense, the slowness of his writing reveals his general attitude of hesitancy and inhibition. He is probably not too successful in his work, for his uncertain strokes express disappointment. He obviously lacks both energy and any glimmering or initiative.

Sample 61. The handwriting of this business woman reveals, through a predominance of the lower loops, her well-trained and practical intelligence, in addition to her independence of thought and action. The letters are individually shaped, and the clear spacing of words reflects her practical intelligence and initiative.

Sample 62. This script is that of a butler and discloses

51

the born servant-one whose exactness and passion for detail are obvious in the minutely formed letters. We can easily see that his dependent mind exists only to receive orders. He will never be able to be his own master.

Sample 63. Here we find the disciplined mind of a school teacher, which expresses itself in a regular spacing of the words. The writing, as a whole, however, shows that the writer is more able to carry out than to issue orders, since he is somewhat lacking in initiative. From the rounded angle we learn that his intellect has not absorbed his emotions, so that he has a comprehension of the child's nature, and should, therefore, be successful in guiding the characters of his students. The steady basic line reveals his firm character and the energy which is present in his instructive ability.

Sample 64. This specimen of handwriting uncovers an energetic woman who has regimented her life and work. She is the head of a social organization, and knows how to deal with many different people. The rounded angle reveals her warm heart, though the backward angle shows that her mind controls her emotions. This woman will never underrate herself, and she is accustomed to giving orders which she expects to be obeyed. The heavy pressure discloses her domineering instinct, while the circles over her 'i','s show her tendency to act and dress extravagantly.

From these different handwritings we learn that the man with practical intelligence is inclined to concentrate his activity on reality and mundane affairs, somewhat neglecting the spiritual and intellectual side of life.

He can only understand factual matters, while abstract sciences, theories, and ideas remain unkown to him.

CHAPTER TEN

THE INTELLECTUAL

Generally speaking, the intellectual is more attracted by cosmic ideas than by the reality of the material world. Endowed with a clear mind and an alert intellect, adapting himself to the requirements of life, he will develop already pioneered sciences through his discoveries which open the way for new horizons. His handwriting reveals his deductive analytical or intuitive ability; though the intellectual who possesses such a quality of mind will frequently have an unquiet nature. His handwriting exhibits more speed and sweep, with a tendency to simplify letters. He will be able, through his penetration, to solve many of the different problems of life. A smaller and more concentrated style of writing betrays an emphasis on detail, observation, and acquisitiveness for knowledge.

We will now examine the handwritings of an engineer, a lawyer, a naturalist, and a physician, men whose professions necessitate practice as well as theory. Preponderance of the upper zone is expressed in the following writings of philosophers, mathematicians, and scientists, indicating their bias toward the world of theory and ideology, and away from that of material things.

Sample 65. Here we see the handwriting of an engineer who is endowed with an alert intellect, and well able to solve practical problems. He writes with more speed than beauty. His rapid and fluid writing shows an able and penetrating intellect. Simplified letters coupled with a rightward angle picture the writer's objectivity: he will perceive the essentials of a problem, and pursue it to a logical conclusion.

Sample 66. This naturalist bases his researches on facts,- his knowledge and discoveries have their foundation in actual experience as well as in scientific theory. This script betrays a clear and objective mind through the use of the rightward angle, evenly spaced words, and simplified letters. His use of very small letters shows that his intelligence has, through patient researches, learned how to take cognizance of the new ideas discovered in his material.

Samples 67, 68 and 69 contain well-connected letters which reveal the logic and deduction of versatile intellects. 68 is a sample of the handwriting of a geologist, and 69 of a physician. The somewhat disconnected writing in sample 67 mirrors the analytic mind of a chemist whose researches are of a detailed nature.

Sample 70. This handwriting, that of a lawyer, exhibits a larger and more disconnected script. Some letters, however, are skillfully connected, betraying the writer's intuitive as well as deductive powers. The continual change in slant uncovers his dexterity in solving difficult problems.

The connection of '*i*' dots and '*a*'s with the following letters reveals a deductive and executive ability. Threadlike terminals always indicate diplomacy, caution, and experience in life, while pointed terminals disclose a critical sense, and well-spaced words a clearness of thought. Disconnected writing with a skillful connection of single letters reveals an intuitive mind, and also an executive ability.

The small and regular letters of *Sample* 71 reveal an intellect which has a tendency to systematize. Exact and minute formation of letters reflects the patient and precise work of this coleopterist who collects his beetles with painstaking exactness, and systematizes and classifies his work with great care. It is interesting to note that some of his letters are shaped like small beetles.

Sample 72. The upper zone predominates in the handwriting of this philosopher. We notice some letters climbing to the higher sphere, while a graceful sway in the formation of the small letters reveals the writer's richness of ideas. The disconnected letters uncover a mind accustomed to a scrutiny of abstract systems. He is especially interested in philosophy and religious philosophy. High flying '*i*' dots refllect idealism and show that his spiritual life dominates his materialistic self.

Sample 73. This handwriting reflects the personal integrity of an independent and original mind, and the disconnected letters show the writer's intuition and reveal the fine soul of an artist. The writer specializes in Asiatic art, music and culture. We notice frequent arabesques in his handwriting, a symbol of his engrossing studies. If the page is turned upside down, these flourishes become even more apparent.

CHAPTER ELEVEN

THE INTUITIVE AND CREATIVE MIND

The inventor, the genius, and the intuitive person will all find new ideas through their investigation of the inscrutable and unknown. The handwriting of these writers exhibits individual and original letter formation. Their creative power reflects a special characteristic, a *visual* third dimension, which gives the reader a sense of perspective through its conspicuous plasticity, and distinguishes this type of script from the more common two dimensional writing.

We shall now investigate the third dimensional handwritings of several highly gifted men.

Wolfgang von Goethe:

Here we observe the harmonious writing of the great poetic genius Wolfgang von Goethe. The writing appears to be moving rhythmically across the page, and through the presence of the third dimension, the reader has the impression of looking deep into the script itself. The abundance of beauty and imaginative power which exists in the unique ornamentations reveal the innate culture and refinement of this genius. The rightward angle betrays his vast comprehension of human nature, and his interest in everything about him. In his picturesque flourishes we see the appreciation for the fine arts which led him to devote one period of his life to drawing and painting.

55

Feruccio Busoni:

The musical and artistic personality of the Italian pianist and composer, Feruccio Busoni, is revealed in the harmony of his writing as a whole, and the beautiful and brush-like strokes of his single letters. His deep comprehension of all the manifestations of beauty, and love for art in its purest forms are expressed in the script which he forms with an inherent sense of proportion. The somewhat regular, though not monotonous angle reflects an unconscious musical rhythm, while his artistic intuition is mirrored in the disconnected letters. The firmness of pressure reveals his capacity for sustained effort and concentration. The capital 'S's with their protective arcs sympolize his ability, not only to create, but also to teach others, and lead them into a true development of their talents. The flourishing tail of the 'i' which underlines his signature reveals his talent for the fine arts.

Edward Mac Dowell:

In Edward Mac Dowell's harmonious script, we find a good example of the musician's sensibility, and the lyric soul of an artist. The fine spacing and good adjustment of the entire writing reveal his aesthetic sense, while the beautiful flourishes reflect his talent for the fine arts. From the dynamic writing, we realize the vitality of his mind; the original formation of his letters mirror his creative powers.

The writing as a whole, reveals the inherent fineness of his personality, and his perseverance and vitality are disclosed in the energetic pressure. His sense of musical color is obvious in the lights and shadows of his writing. It seems obvious that this writer is a fine lyric tone poet, rather than a dramatic composer. The writing is simple and clear, lacking in artificial effects, letters growing upwards into the upper zone reveal a spirit which, rising over the heaviness of the world, finds its true expression in aesthetic harmony.

Thomas Mann:

The handwriting of the novelist Thomas Mann re-

56

produces the author's talent for aesthetic detail. His intense intellect and idealism are expressed in the minute and characteristically shaped letters, while his artistry finds realization in the unusual formation of his capitals. This writer has a highly concentrated and intuitive nature, coupled with a broad comprehension of humanity. The characteristically falling endings of the words express his tendency to expound a pessimistic ideology.

Darius Milhaud:

The script of Darius Milhaud, like his music, tends to be more dramatic than lyric. The abandonment of his isolated initials and the verve of his writing as a whole are parallel to the vital facility of his compositions. The swift stroke over his signature is an outward manifestation of his general assurance of his place as a revolutionary composer.

André Gide:

This is the handwriting of the French author André Gide. His great literary talent and innate culture are most apparent in this script. His original and artistic personality finds its expression in his use of the third dimension, which also characterizes his foresight and imaginative power. His love of form is mirrored in the intricately designed loops of the upper and lower zone, while his fondness of nature appears in his pasty pressure. The high '*i*' dots, or in this case, commas, show his imagination and sense of humor. His ease of expression is indicated by what we call the 'literary' formation of his '*d*'s a formation which turns back upon itself.

Claude Debussy:

The French composer Claude Debussy repeats in his writing the impressionistic period in music, with which he is closely identified. Some features of romanticism are still visible in his sensitiveness to color, which takes the form of light and shade in his script. The diminutive elegance of this writing is due to the writer's musical impressions, as well as the influence of French impressionist painting and poetry. There is no passion or deep feeling to be seen in this script—only lyric refinement. The plasticity of the third dimension reveals his irrefutable genius.

Maurice Ravel:

Here is a certain affinity in the characters, expression, and conception of *Debussy* and *Ravel*. While we observe a somewhat effeminate delicacy in Debussy, we see in Ravel a stronger rhythmical backbone, a more realistic, forceful and masculine type of script, uncovered by the relatively heavy pressure of his pen. This script shows great creative power, and we see that the letters are formed with a great sense of clarity and plasticity. The boldness of his musical compositions, the ardor of his temperament, and the fertility of his creative power are all visible in the capital S's, and especially in the innumerable musical symbols present in this script. The even pressure shows his energy and unique sense of musical color. The upper zone predominates, but the lower is well developed, showing the balance of his vital reality.

Hendrik Willem van Loon:

The light, firm strokes and third dimensional perspective show van Loon's strong intuitive sense, while the dashes which occasionally connect one word with the next reveal his practical intelligence. It is interesting to see how in this letter, as in all of his works themselves, he cannot divorce pictures from the written word- and even the words themselves look like minute sketches. The caricature over the signature displays van Loon's affable self-assurance. A man who decorates his correspondence with such sensitively humorous pictures reveals his ability to win the confidence and affection of the majority of the people with whom be comes in contact.

CHAPTER TWELVE

LYING AND DISSIMULATION

It is of great importance that we must realize the part which untruthfulness plays in the relationship of one person to another; since there are many different forms of sincerity and insincerity. At times, the child takes pleasure in inventing stories, whether he does this to defend himself from punishment, or only because he confuses fact and imagination. The adult, not admitting his bad habits or shortcomings, tries to embellish certain weak points in his character so that he may make a good impression on others.

One person lies to protect himself from the criticism of stronger individuals, the weakling to avoid making a decision, the lazy person as an excuse for his easy-going life, the vain to impress others, the greedy for material advantage, and so on.

We shall begin with the lies of the child. Oftimes children show an abundance of exaggerated imagination, and are unable to distinguish between actual fact and their own fancies. Because of this confusion, they are not reliable witnesses in such situations as court inquiries, etc. In other cases, the child lies for fear of punishment. Not all parents and teachers have a proper comprehension of the child's nature. The child feels himself unprotected in the face of the adult's authority, and tries to defend himself against what he believes to be unreasonable harshness, by resorting to lies.

In normal cases, these weaknesses in the child's character disappear during the time of adolescence. Pathological cases, however, will be discussed in a later chapter.

Sample 74. Misunderstanding and a too severe education have turned this fourteen-year-old girl into a liar. She is lazy and often absent-minded, absorbed in her own more pleasant pursuits. The confused and wavering writing shows that she has little will-power, and that she defends herself by lying in order to avoid punishment, since she is indiscriminately punished for everything, even for such minor faults as untidiness in her books and clothing, and negligence in accomplishing her tasks. The shaky script and uneven pressure mirror her sloppiness, and weakness of character. The small letters placed between larger ones picture her fear of punishment. Her relatively steady capital letters reflect her fear and opposition of those adults whose attitude seems, to her, to be both unfriendly and unreasonable. This girl is in constant need of excuses, whether they are for her laziness, negligence, or general carelessness in her duties in school or at home. Due to parental mismanagement and her own negative reaction to it, she is always forced to be on the alert in her invention of stories.

Sample 75. The unequal writing in the script of this eleven-year-old boy reflects his repressed character and general reserve, while, the angular style of writing coupled with the closed vowels emphasize this fact. We notice some rounded letters which indicate his affection and sensibility. This child simultaneously admires and envies his older brother, to whom he feels deeply inferior since he believes him to be exceptionally strong and gifted. The boy tries, however, to conceal his sensibility, for he wants to appear invincible in the eyes of his playmates, and is afraid to be teased because of his femineity. He has many innocent secrets, and displays a strangely pedantic attitude which is apparent in a script which looks somewhat like a length of barbed wire.

Sample 76. The writing of this girl of fifteen reveals an extremely sensual imagination. The large and angular lower loops uncover her effusive nature, while leftward traits indicate that she takes refuge in dreams from the monotony of her daily life. The slow traits indicate her laziness and, as a consequence, her neglected or unaccomplished assignments. We notice, however, in a few uniquely formed letters, that she has great hopes for her future. She uses her lively imagination to conceal character deficiencies with such probability and participation in these fabrications, that she eventually believes these stories herself.

Sample 77. The author of this writing is a woman of over 51 whose extreme imagination is revealed in the long lower loops. She lacks discipline in her daily life, and finds it hard to stick to extensive work, for she is aimless and uneconomical. On the one hand she is too generous in her spending, depriving herself of necessities so that she may be able to lavish gifts on her friends, on the other, she finds herself unhappy when she is forced to manage with insufficient means. It is obvious that she does not know how to face hardships, or even reality, for she takes an oblivious refuge in a dream world. Though such an amount of imagination should form a basis for a creative life, in this woman, however, it is merely a block in her personality development. This obstacle is very apparent in her futile flourishes, and the inconsistently large letters at the beginning of each word.

These different examples prove that it is not easy to distinguish between sincerity and untruthfulness. Only that individual who has reached spiritual maturity, and who has concentrated his energies in an active altruism, can be called sincere. The man who is sincere in his attitude towards himself will be able to act sincerely with others, since he is motivated by self-knowledge.

Sample 78. This handwriting belongs to a fifty-year-old woman, whose letters are so childishly formed that we might think that they had been written by a very young person. The script, as a whole, appears to have been written by an undeveloped and infantile character. The school model is entirely preserved, and betrays the writer's narrow-mindedness and arrested development. The closed vowels reveal her secretive and evasive nature, which makes it impossible for her to manage her life.

Sample 79. This sample of the script of a thirty-three-year-old woman shows her to be a repressed and reserved personality. Her real being is enclosed behind the conventionally formal attitude of a society woman. We notice her prudence and constraint in the small, pinched letters, while her wish to appear serene and in command is expressed in the high and ascending letters. She watches herself carefully, displaying an artificial and insincere attitude. In spite of this, however, she feels out of place, and even suffers from a strong inferiority complex. Although she is talented and endowed with innate culture and good taste, she is unable to make use of her various gifts. Her continual dissimulation has upset her nervous system, making it extremely delicate; she complains of different ailments, which, although she herself has created them, keep her from enjoying her life.

Sample 80. An artificiality coupled with leftward involved traits characterizes this egotistic woman, who attaches significance to her pleasures and personal success alone. The connected letters reveal her adaptability to circumstances. Pretension and affectation are mirrored in this writing, but we see that the writer is adept at making an immediate connection with other people. We notice that the letters and even the words are wedge-shaped, revealing her dissimulation and egocentricity. An ordinary mind, though theatrical, reflecting only average intelligence, is expressed in this writing.

Sample 81. This writing reflects a strange combination of vain imperiousness and insufficiency which exists in the thirty-eight-year-old woman, who is consistently deceiving herself and others. Her most dangerous propensities are materialistic greed and extreme ambition. We discover her self-centered character in the narrow and angular traits, while her greed comes to light in the fat lower loops. The innumerable flourishes mirror her exaggeration of imagination and sentiment. Though she possesses practical intelligence, we can see an arrested development in some of her tangled and infantile flourishes. She tries to conceal her inadequacy in a plethora of words which she hopes will attract attention to herself. She is able to change her characterization as the occasion seems to demand, when she detects a negative attitude in others.

Sample 82. This is the handwriting of a male homosexual. The leftward traits and garlands fading away into threads, uncover the repressed character of a man who has learned how to conceal those desires and passions which are opposed to the general mores of society. In his script, we see that the vowels are sometimes partially unclosed, showing a certain dissimulation which is for him self-defense. In addition to these traits, we notice a certain arrested development which is expressed in childish traits and psychic infantility.

Sample 83. Passions and concealed sexual desires predominate in the handwriting of this twenty-six-year-old woman, manifesting themselves in broken-back lower loops. The abrupt changes in the slant of her writing prove her to be extremely volatile; one day she wishes to become an artist, on another a scientist. On one occasion she can work with perseverance, while within the next twenty-four hours she has lost her interest in everything but dreaming. She is absolutely unreliable, both in accomplishing her work and in keeping her promises, since her moods are based on capricious whims. She has enough ability to succeed in almost any career, but her laziness impedes any development in her talents. In order to conceal her weakness this writer invents stupid lies. She sees no reason for paying attention to the ideas of her friends, since she believes that her opinion, alone, is worthy of being taken seriously. In the falling ending we see the disappointment which is a logical consequence of her egocentricity.

In addition to those neurotically unstable individuals who can never act with complete sincerity, there are others who suffer from organic rather than psychic handicaps, and therefore approach everything in a negative manner. They regard healthy people with a bitter dislike, and are discontented not only with the world, but themselves as well. We find that such characters, unhappy in themselves, do not want their fellow-beings to be any happier.

63

Sample 84.   This handwriting belongs to a twenty-two-year-old college student.   From her early childhood, she has had a hard struggle for her daily needs.   This sense of privation, plus the fact that she was brought up without affection, has left a deteriorating impression on her mind, and she feels generally disgusted and isolated.   The narrow angle in a rather large writing reflects this lack of feeling and affection towards herself as well as others.   Though she is endowed with many unusual gifts, she does not trust other people, and envies those individuals who seem to her to be more fortunate.   The rightward and rapid writing, coupled with long lower loops, reveal her materialistic wishes and her ambition to make her own way for herself. The insincerity of this girl is a result of necessity rather than preference.

CHAPTER   THIRTEEN

THE HANDWRITING OF THE CRIMINAL

Through the study of all types of individuals, we find that the kind of failure which causes criminals is similar to that which results in problem children, suicides, drunkards, and sexual perverts, as well as in neurotics and psychotics. They all fail in both their approach and their adjustment to life, and above all they are unified in their lack of social interest, and any form of creative cooperation.

Even here, however, we cannot distinguish between these individuals and those who are considered "normal": there are no born criminals.   No one person can be held up as an example of perfect cooperation or perfect social conscientiousness, and those with criminal tendencies have only failed more drastically than is usual.   There is no true compulsion in either environment or heredity: children from the same family and environment can and do develop in different ways.   Sometimes a criminal type appears in a family of irreproachable record, and inversely a family with a very poor record sometimes produces children of good

64

character and behavior. It happens, too, that some criminals change in later life, and criminologists have often been hard put to explain how a burgler may settle down, at the height of his maturity, and become a useful citizen. If crime were an inborn defect, or if it were indelibly imposed by the environment, we could not be able to understand such improvement.

A series of varied samples of handwritings will help to explain how the demands of life and the mistakes in fulfilling them are apt to bring criminal charateristics to the surface, rendering such individuals helpless to save themselves. They are not inherently responsible; their crimes are the result of their complete failure to understand and adjust to society's restrictions.

Character is not fixed, but is always a fine and complicated structure which yields to the influence of thousands of external and internal pressures. Misery and the demands of necessity are at times responsible for an unfavorable development of any character. A weak and pliable nature gives way to destructive influences more easily than a firm and steady one.

Sample 85. This sample is written by a girl of fourteen, the daughter of a laborer who has a very low social and moral standard. Her teachers report that she is vain, egotistic and untruthful, and is lazy and undutiful. Her exhibitionism and domineering nature are discovered in occasional heavy down strokes, while the sharp, angular style expresses her ¹ack of consideration. Her weak will is expressed in the wavering pressure and slant; and the slowly written and unequally spaced words and letters, show her laziness and poor sense of duty. While the stumpy lower loops indicate gluttony, and especially a precocious sensuality, the whole writing appears to be the work of a much younger child. She conceals her indolence with lies and dissimulation which are expressed in broken back and involved letters. This handwriting is a combination of the three components of a fraudulent character: idleness, vanity, and gluttony. This girl attaches importance to

65

herself alone: the lack of development in her social consciousness is due, in all probability, to her unfavorable environment.

Sample 86.   This is the handwriting of a convict who specializes in rifling luggage in trains.   The relatively slow writing reveals the laziness of a person who prefers to make money in the easiest possible way.   The leftward flourishes are written with practiced agility, and are graphic symbols of the technique of this thief, who could steal with rapidity and inconspicuousness.   His leftward flourishes take the shape of snares, symbolizing his criminal tendencies.

Sample 87.   Here, again, we see the skillful leftward flourishes whose endings are formed like slings.   This man has committed far greater thefts than the train robber of Sample 86, acting in a shrewder and more original manner. His specialty is stealing diamonds.   He has been imprisoned several times, but, immediately upon release, he repeats the pattern which his criminality has assumed.

While thieves are not always social parasites, they are morally unsound, and their writing vacillates with weak and uneven pressure, denoting the average petty thief, such as the pickpocket or small swindler.   The thief who robs banks, counterfeits, or perpetrates a large-scale swindle, is one of two types: either he is aggressive and material, writing with heavy pressure and close connecting strokes, as in Sample 87, or he is a leader in the great criminal world, where he has found expression for his drive for personal power.

Sample 88.   This handwriting is surprising in its pleasing formation, and the clear spacing of words which betray the forty-year-old writer's clarity of ideas.   This man displays logic, reason and a talent for accounting.   He has an exceptionally charming personality, excellent manners, and a fine appearance: he is a swindler on a grand scale. The heavy terminals, flung downwards into a hook, indicate his aggressiveness and obstinacy.   His deceptions take the form of introducing himself as a prince, and gain-ing the confidence of his victims through his amiability and and persuasion, thus paving the way for his borrowing large sums of money, only to vanish into thin air. The large and graceful flourishes mirror his self-confidence and arrogance. The initial letters reveal great presence of mind and a tremendous amount of aggressive vitality.

Society is endangered by the duplicity of such criminals as swindlers and confidence men, who conceal their true nature behind a mask of honesty. We find a typical example of this criminal group posing as a respectable employee who fulfills his duties faithfully, while he is planning to take full advantage of his trusted position. Again, we see that the irreproachable behavior of the pupil on whom the teacher invariably relies, conceals a personality which secretly gratifies every corrupt desire. While these types seem to adapt themselves admirably to social life, or rather to its exploitation, they really have no interest either in cooperation, or in anything that is not to their advantage. These people are very difficult to unmask because their honesty and industriousness appear to be unshakably genuine. We know of cases where a man has spent many years of continued and successful frauds which did not excite the least suspicion in anyone, and whose treachery was only detected by accident.

Sample 89. Through its uniform regularity, this script characterizes the above mentioned attitude of guilt. This fifty-year-old director of an insurance company has embezzled huge funds over many years of apparently conscientious service, and has been detected only through the analysis of handwriting. Paradoxically, the regularity of his writing reveals him to be a diligent man who accomplishes his daily tasks with a great sense of duty. His value as a superior worker is revealed in the high capital letters; he knows how to conduct his business with tact, and inspires great confidence. His letters are written with incredible regularity, while the long lower loops of the capital letter *B* uncover his materialistic drive for money and possessions. Beneath his pose of trustworthiness, we can observe many graphic examples of dissimulation in the very narrow angle of crowded and involved vowels. The letters which are formed with an up and down stroke, as *f, b,* and *h,* are painstakingly retraced so that their natural loops become a cramped and continuous line- a gesture typical of veiled deception. A neurotic anxiety and constant fear of discovery are reflected in the narrow and rigid writing. Although he carried off the fraud with such secrecy that it was exceedingly difficult to convict him, his neurotic fears prevented him from enjoying his success. The handwriting typifies not only the deceptive-criminal type, but also a materialistic and selfish personality.

Sample 90. The initial letters of many words reveal the writer's arrogance, while the garlands uncover the evasive nature of a man who successfully conceals his real intentions and desires. Some letters which are hardly legible,—the capital '*t*'s and '*v*'s are easily confused—and the numerous involved traits reflect his moral turpitude. The heavy pressure typifies his great strength of personality and power of suggestion which attract people to him, and make them an easy prey. The sharpness of the letters gives the reader a most unpleasant impression of this sensual man, and the long descending loops testify to his brutal nature and violent passions.

This is the handwriting of a forty-year-old director of a musical institute and college for girls which he established and financed with funds which he had fraudulently solicited. This institute was only a pretext for his realization of a perverted and uncontrollable sensuality. Choosing only those girls who had weak and servile characters, he maintained this school for the sole purpose of ravishing his "pupils", whom he kept there at their own wish by presents and compliments. He was able to conduct this scheme with so much skill until he was denounced by a girl and given a severe sentence only after years of blatant activity.

Criminality is almost always a psychopathic tendency. At this point, it is well to realize that the graphologist must carefully investigate all writing of abnormal proportions, where the letter formation is nevertheless completely usual. Thus, extreme expansion or contraction, in an otherwise undistinguished writing, is an indication of some serious mental abnormality. In contrast to the normally proportionate formation and size of letters, we can see that, for example, the combination of sharply disconnected letters and a preponderance of the upper zone in a very small script, is an exaggerated example of the case at hand. Again, a totally undistinguished writing whose size is abnormally exaggerated or minimized reveals delusions which easily lead to criminal action.

Sample 91. The flourishes which we see in the sample are signs of exaggerated feelings, while the spasmodic increase of pressure reveals the writer's violent reactions to every emotional stimulus, and his sharpened endings show aggressiveness and violence. Inconsistent traits show his lack of control, and the wavering basic line reveals sudden changes in mood, with a basic depression and discontent.

This writer belongs in the cicloid group, which corresponds with Jung's extrovert. He is weak, impressionable, and extremely emotional. Acting upon every stimulus and impulse, he is easily swayed by the superabundance of impetuous feelings and desires. As a result, his emotional life is restless and unstable. When he was thirty, he culminated a furious scene of jealousy by threatening his sweetheart with a revolver. When she tried to escape by jumping out of the window, he lost the little control which he had left, and killed her. Some minutes later his mood changed from frenzy to despair, and he commited suicide.

The schizoid type, corresponding with Jung's introvert, is unsociable and unadaptable. Many schizoids appear indifferent towards everything; some are indolent or phlegmatic, and others dispassionately cruel, but this type, though apathetic and even indolent, sometimes shows great anger and violence. On the other hand, there are schizoids who

69

commit dreadful atrocities with incredible heartlessness, and a total lack of any normal feelings.

The schizoid's unsociability and his criminal propensities are often manifested in his early childhood, through his resentful unmanageability and his total refusal to study, or plan for a future career. Schizoids display a hostile reserve in their relationships, and tend to prefer an easy and vagabond life, unhampered by personal bonds, in which they can prosper through fraud and robbery. As children, they show no affection whatever for parents and relatives, and any slight inconvenience may provoke brutal and violent reactions.

Sample 92. The handwriting of this schizoid type belongs to a man of thirty. It is slow and the childish letters are formed with a leftward angle. This writer never studied anything thoroughly, and has no idea of the meaning of the word duty. Since childhood, he has led a lazy and self-indulgent life, stealing money to make this feasible. The sharp, angular writing together with a leftward angle shows him to be a man who goes his own way recklessly without accepting any guidance, and will not adapt himself to society. The heavy *t* bars and smeary pressure mirror his violence and mental unbalance, while the pointed angular style indicates his cruelty.

Sample 93. The sharp and ugly traits of this sample are graphic symbols of the writer's aggressive destruction. This man is dishonest and cannot be trusted with anything. The fact that he is deceitful, cunning, evasive and conceals his real personality is revealed in his poorly defined letters. He is unbalanced and an extremist, a cicloid who at the time of writing this sample was undergoing a typical state of sensual elation. He is negatively over-sexed and has a perverted imagination. He is, however, intelligent enough to know how to avoid detection. He is obviously abnormal, and totally lacking any moral sense. If caught in a lie he will baldly assert that he has been misunderstood. Since he is excitable, he lacks self-control and any

70

sense of responsibility. At one time he was convicted of brutal rape.

In the handwritings of murderers, we frequently find characteristic shapes which symbolize their basic tendency to kill. Cesare Lombroso, the Italian scientist, was the first to write a book on the handwriting of the criminal, reproducing the signatures of murderers which flaunt the terrible symbols of blood and death.

Sample 94. The slowness with which this sample was written reveals the girl's laziness and indolence, while the muddy pressure betrays her concealed but ardent sensuality. The long lower loops reveal her materiality- the double closed vowels her dissimulation and untruthfulness. There is no true vitality in this writing. The smeary pressure discloses a definitely psychopathic disposition. The father of this twenty-five-year-old girl was a brutal and violent drunkard. In this script, we notice some signs of her mental degeneration which has taken the form of a decline in intelligence, insensibility and apathy, as well as a sudden and aggressive temper, a mind closed to education, and un-restrained sexual desires. An only child, she was brought up in different countries. She has always been totally in-sincere, even with her mother, who had recently divorced the girl's father and remarried. The girl had no connect-ion with either her mother or her step-father, and, hating to be under any obligation to them, stole money for her expenses, though she lived in a luxurious home. This is a marked characteristic of a hysterical personality, where the subject would rather behave like a criminal than allow himself to be discommoded in any way. This girl indulged in many affairs which she conducted in her mother's house. When she was discovered with one of her lovers, she ran away, only to be found, after a long search, in a sanatorium where she had been confined by the local authorities because of her pronounced mental condition.

Psychiatry devotes a great part of its studies to the psychopathic epileptic character. The physical manifestations are far more pronounced and perverse than those of the 'normal' epileptic.

Sample 95.   This epileptic man, transported by an impetuous and uncontrollable sexual desire, attacked a girl in broad daylight and raped her publicly, unable to consider the obvious consequences.   His writing is very unequal and tangled.   Wavering lines and senselessly involved traits which resemble superimposed letters mirror his confusion, and the heavy horizontal strokes reflect his insane violence.   The entangled letters symbolize a mind which is unable to reason out the simplest problems.   The writer lacks any sense of judgment, can only vaguely comprehend a small part of life, and is unable to profit by even the most drastic experience.   The unsteady traits with light pressure reflect the weakness of his will-power.   Lacking in self-control, he yields to every impulse and thought, while the irritability is revealed by the sporadic pressure.

This thirty-year-old pervert could only finish elementary school, and was supported by his relatives.   When questioned as to the motive behind his crimes, he only grins stupidly.

Alcoholism has a destructive influence on the character, weakening the will-power and intelligence, and increasing emotional excitability.   The drunkard neglects his family obligations and tries his best to avoid regular work which requires any responsibility.   This vice weakens the drinker's moral sense, and certainly leads him to corruption.

Sample 96.   This thirty-four-year-old woman has been confined in an insane asylum because of a fit of drunkenness in which she injured several members of her family.   Her rising pathological excitement is revealed in an abnormal pressure; the down strokes of the terminal *r*, especially in the word 'for', uncover her unrestrained violence.   The unequal traits and the slant both ways reflect her deficient will-power and lack of self-control.   The slow and disconnected letters, which are immaturely formed, look as though they had been written by a child.   The whole writing is unsteady and trembling, showing the writer's pronounced lassitude, and slow and distracted thoughts. Her memory is unsure and fragmentary. This deficiency of will-power, intelligence and emotional stability has turned the writer into a most deplorable individual. Her unrestrainable violence has caused so much danger both to herself and to others that she cannot yet be released from the asylum.

Sample 97. shows another criminal case caused by alcoholism. This handwriting contains regular traits and graceful and individually shaped letters. It is written by an educated and intelligent woman. The continual change of slant, however, together with the smeary pressure and wavering basic line uncover her unrestrainable desire for liquor. She was divorced by her husband because he considered her an unfit mother for their child. Although his accusation was entirely justified, she exaggerated her unhappiness, and aroused local resentment against her husband. During an argument, she became so enraged that she threw a heavy object at him which, had she not missed, might have killed him. Because of this incident, her husband forced her to leave the community.

Unnatural quarrels in the family circle lead some individuals to harbor feelings of resentment and desperation. Hate can lead to cruelty and vengeance, but in order to commit any criminal act, there must always be an acquired criminal disposition.

Sample 98. This is the handwriting of a farmer's widow who, until she was fifty, worked hard and dutifully to support her family. Her relationship with her daughter-in-law was, however, very strained, especially over the question of an impending inheritance. Because of this ill-feeling, she carried tales of the daughter's misbehavior to all her neighbors. This enmity was not, however, pronounced enough to justify her unpredictably violent revenge upon the young woman.

One morning as her daughter-in-law left communion,

this woman met her at the church door with a vindictive diatribe, at the end of which she drew a knife and stabbed the girl.

The large and unequal handwriting with long, pointed traits reveals her intense irritability, violence, and lack of self-control. The abnormally uneven pressure reveals a constantly increasing excitability, probably provoked by menopause, or some other disturbance.

Many such criminal acts as those mentioned above have their origin in what the individual calls 'difficult and adverse life', such as continued unemployment or a miserable social standard of life. These people, having nothing to hold on to, neither a faith in God nor in themselves, become criminals.

Sample 99. This is the handwriting of another quite different case of a forty-three-old lawyer who, on an impulse, left his office and embarked on a pleasure trip with the money entrusted to him by his clients. Since he had always been an honest and reliable man, this unpremeditated act was not the result of criminal tendencies, but the sudden manifestation of a progressive and general paresis. The pasty pressure together with unequal and disconnected traits and a wavering basic line reflect the writer's diseased mind. While paresis often manifests itself in confused and extravagant impulses, in this case, however, it developed secretly until this final outburst. The senselessly disconnected letters show the writer's confusion.

From these many samples of handwriting, we can see the multiple reasons which are the basis of a criminal life. Gradual deficiency of the character, physical and mental abnormalities, and most of all any basic moral weakness can produce a criminal type. Every day our newspapers are full of reported crimes, of children who have been abandoned or, even worse, oppressed and warped by a corrupt environment. These poor youngsters, kept from a positive development, often become a danger to the community.

74

Delusions of grandeur can also lead to criminality. A careful study of the handwriting of many notorious criminals will show how much tragedy could have been avoided if the criminal disposition had been discovered and re-channeled before it had a chance to take tangible form.

In studying the script of a man who has surprised society by becoming a criminal at an advanced age, the graphologist can trace the gradual rise of what have always been latent criminal tendencies, but which have, until the last, been constrained.

In dealing with the criminal problem in general, the graphologist must not be prejudiced by the pressure of public hysteria. In order to explain even the most atrocious murder, we must accept the fact that our thoughts are the most vital factors in our lives, and that they are the basis for all actions. Thoughts are things, they are the lever with which we can control circumstances. The detailed history of any murderer will show that the handwriting never lies. It contains special characteristics which clearly reveal what will happen when this writer comes face to face with adverse circumstances.

The graphologist is forced to take the attitude of many philosophers and psychologists, that a great many criminal acts are only explosions of energy which are disastrous in their misdirection. If we knew the former history of many a criminal we might be able to determine just how he came to his present plight. We perhaps might perceive how a kind word or a loving deed at the beginning of his career could have halted him and turned him to a career of usefulnes and success. Most people go wrong because they seem to lack the incentive to go to the right direction, either because of wrong education in early years or because of wrong example.

CHAPTER FOURTEEN

HANDLING THE SUPERSENSITIVE

Freud based his school of thought on sexual instinct and problems, without placing sufficient importance on any of the other instincts which often contribute to nervousness, arrested development, and a state of repression.

Alfred Adler, the pupil of Freud, mainly stresses the drive for power, but he particularly emphasizes the roots of all evil which are grown in early childhood. The child is aware of the fact that he is physically and mentally inferior to the adult. Often even small defeats and humiliations arouse in him a feeling of impotence and inferiority. In addition to these, innate physical weakness may aggravate the child's feeling of insufficiency. The adult's lack of indulgence and comprehension can intensify the child's sense of conflict at a very early age. The first memories play an important part in Adler's research. He asserts: "With a feeling of inferiority which has increased through the passing years, the youth also increases a desire to demonstrate his self-confidence. He wants to impose his personality upon the environment which he has learned to dominate".

A feeling of inferiority may cause such nervous disturbance in a child as stammering or facial tics, as well as forcing him to indulge in making faces, and performing other such exhibitionistic naughtiness. Often a child, thinking himself neglected, will try to attract the attention and affection of his family by pretending to be sick.

Carl Jung evolves a conception of the subconscious where the individual and the collective subconscious are two distinct entities. The first includes all remote desires and memories, remnants of the child's personality. The second, however, penetrates into the recesses of the child's soul where the pictures and experiences of all times and generations are stored. Jung says: "The collective subconscious is a vessel which contains all traces of the universal subconscious, all memories of archaic and mythological imagination- the noblest sentiments and discoveries, as well as the half-remembered trauma-hence it is the source of all human feelings, and of all creative impulses. The most precious of life's treasures are concealed here in their profundity."

In addition to Jung's types, the extrovert and the introvert, he distinguishes four fundamental mental functions: perception, feeling, reason, and intuition. In regard to the degree of adaptability he lists the selfish, the sensitive, the reasoner, and the intuitive. The selfish person is involved in his own feelings and ideas; the sensitive is almost entirely dominated by the acuteness of his emotions. The reasoner weighs the world with his critical perception; and the intuitive foresees and prepares himself for future events and new potentialities. All four types can be either extrovert or introvert.

There are, however, characters whose moods change for no tangible reason. Certain temperaments tend to maintain alternating emotional states which make them see the world in contrasting lights, sometimes gay and full of hope, at others black and depressing. The source of their moods cannot be traced to pleasant or unpleasant happenings, but exists in the individual's basic tendency towards exaltation or melancholy, indolence or emotional excitability. The neurasthenic, the hysteric, the cicloid and the schizoid form the four divisions of this unstable type.

By neurasthenic we mean an individual who is governed by an irritable weakness in his nervous system. A state of weariness and exhaustion is typical of the neurasthenic, weakening his capacity for work through severe depressions. He attaches a hysterical importance to any slight ailment, believing himself stricken with an incurable disease.

Sample 100. The soft, light and unequal script reveals the writer's deficient energy, feelings of insufficiency, and

77

instability of character. Some letters are broken back, while others slope to the right, disclosing his inward struggle against disquietude and repression, in contrast to his active impulses and states of exaltation, showing him to have a personality which fluctuates between lassitude and ardent desires. Some hesitant traits mirror hypochondria. This man's momentary activity is paralyzed by the recurring attacks of weariness and irresolution. His instability of will-power and affections is always surprising to everyone.

Sample 101. The light uneven pressure in the handwriting of this thirty-eight-year-old man indicates his latent, but at present controlled, neurasthenia. While the light and uneven pressure and very short lower loops reveal his extreme sexual apathy, we can observe his excitability, and sudden attacks of weariness and ill temper, expressed in the unequal traits and periodic pressure. He is very intelligent, well educated and versatile, but lacks courage and an optimistic drive.

Sample 102. This is the script of a thirty-year-old journalist. It reveals his gradually acquired sexual neurasthenia, while his heavy horizontal pressure shows an active tendency towards homosexuality. In spite of his well - developed and aesthetic intellect, the script discloses his general feeling of despondency. The extreme contrast between his states of excitability and exhaustion are the consequences of his continual struggle against what he pessimistically considers to be adverse conditions. His energetic interest in his work can vanish suddenly (we notice the angularity fading out into the thread): in such moments of weariness and exhaustion, any slight task, even the strain of having to talk, seems to be a greater trial than he can bear. The graphic signs of his lassitude and depression are the falling endings, and a sudden pressure on occasional strokes, which also reflects his irritability. This kind of neurasthenia can be healed through complete rest, and especially by a thorough examination and renovation of the victim's thoughts and attitude.

The graphic signs of elation are a very large loose writing, with inflated loops and flourishes, and ascending lines. Depression is expressed in hesitant writing, where the words dwindle away into thread-like finals, and descending lines and narrow loops. The tendency to weariness and fatigue appears in the very low *i* dots. Emotinoal excitability is expressed in unequal letters, a sharpened angular style, and sudden pressure on occasional strokes.

Sample 103. The handwriting of this woman discloses the expansive and very lively nature of a cicloid. Periods of increased energy and initiative are followed by days of discouragement and depression. The large and loose writing reveals her easy impressionability, and interest in the life about her. She reacts too readily and with violence to every stimulus of the external and internal worlds, while her moods change suddenly. The unequalness of the whole writing indicates her obvious nervous sensibility and emotional unbalance.

Sample 104. This is the writing of a pianist, a very sensitive musician of great genius, who is, however, unstable and easily impressed. The swift and fluent writing, full of romantic flourishes, mirrors his exaggerated feelings, speech, and action, as well as the richness of his ideas, and his great initiative and activity. The script reflects momentary depression which is expressed in the falling endings and sloping lines. His life has been depressingly full of adversity, and he feels discouraged at the present time, though he is generally affable, and courageously optimistic.

The beautiful and harmonious formation of his letters, together with the unusual word connection, reveals his intuition and creative vitality. In his happy moments, this artist creates with originality and imagination, though, at times, he may be too enthusiastic, and fired by too many ideas at one time as shown by the wavering basic line. He is affectionate, warm hearted, and gregarious. From periods of great activity he will suddenly relapse into weariness and melancholy. In such states of depression, he is unable to work, feels sad and disappointed, and even avoids all contact with his friends. Fortunately, however, these periods of melancholy and introspection do not last very long.

Sample 105. This handwriting is typical of a passively melancholy cicloid temperament. It is the writing of an unreasonably pliant and impressionable woman. The falling endings and lines reflect her tendency to emphasize the dark and unfavorable periods of her life. The slow traits which slope backwards disclose her indolence and lack of initiative. Her pronoun '*I*' shows that she is totally involved in her petty interests, and while always discouraged and disappointed, is avidly interested in what other people think of her. She lacks the will-power to make the most of her life.

These three samples show the strong, alternating tendencies towards depression, passivity, and exaggerated enthusiasm, which place their writers in the cicloid group.

The schizoid reacts entirely different. While he may seem almost phlegmatic in his reactions to certain stimuli, he is surprisingly aroused by others. He harbors grudges for an abnormally long time, and his sour reticence keeps him from making friends. Through his brooding, he creates an electric state of nervous tension which suddenly explodes in a shower of unreasonable complaints and reproaches, creating a most difficult and alienating atmossphere.

Sample 106. The writing of this fifty-year-old woman reveals her aesthetic nature. The narrow, angular style mirrors her unsociable character, while the light, uneven pressure shows her moody temperament. Although the rightward angle reveals her passionate feelings, the narrowness of her letters reflects her self-contained attitude. She dislikes close personal contact, and prefers concealment to confidence. She is always in a state of tension, constantly reviewing her defeats and disappointments-those of many months ago or more recent times- until her feelings burst out in a violent display of temper and acid criticism. This irritability and sarcasm is revealed in her sharp angular style and pointed endings. While she is a gifted musician and dancer, her long low loops reveal not only her well-disciplined coordination, but also her materiality.

This script shows the contrast between her receptive sensibility and her cold reserve, between her brusque attitude and secret dreams. Her nature is distinctly split into halves, divided between her ego and the external world.

The pattern of the hysteric's vagaries differs with the personality involved. We will here discuss only those manifestations which pertain to the hysterical character's inconsistent state of mind, and not go into the pathological manifestations of the true hysteria. While the latter's attacks interrupt a usually normal life, the more generally hysterical individual has an even distribution of his weakness in all his actions and reactions. Typical of the hysterical character is an exaggeration of emotion and enthusiasm, and a rapid transubstantiation of unfavorable occurrences into organic illness. Mental suffering is easily transformed into physical disturbances. In most cases, hysterical symptoms and various organic disturbances are the individual's only weapon by which he can threaten and eventually obtain a change in his environment.

The main symptoms of the hysterical character are extreme egotism, exhibitionism, and a superficial efficiency which conceals only average abilities. Added to these are untruthfulness, secrecy, deception of the self as well as others, extreme excitability, and a general instability.

Infantilism and arrested development are often based on major defects, as well as oversensibility of the nervous system, and a low sexual drive.

The handwriting of the hysterical character is composed of large movements of the pen, and is an artificial writing full of many futile flourishes which are a sign of theatricality. The confused, unequal traits, with their threadlike finals, indicate weakness of character; broken back strokes with large and involved letters mirror the exaggerated imagination which produces lies and dissimulation.

81

Sample 107. One glance at this sample is sufficient to reveal the artificial writing with futile flourishes, typical of the self-dramatization and pretension of a hysterical character, while the broad loops of such letters as *d, l,* or *t,* show the woman's intensely sensitive nature. The backward slopes symbolize her selfishness, and the loops of the '*f*' and '*t*' bars are conspicuous signs of her sybaritic and exhibitionistic nature.

The writer is a woman of thirty, whose one desire is to attract attention to herself, no matter what means she may have to employ. She complains of intense headaches, for which she consults many different kinds of doctors, but no one has succeeded in finding the cause of her complaints. When she feels disappointed or realizes that she must accomplish an unpleasant and unselfish duty, she is immediately stricken with a migraine. She wants to be comforted and pampered, and have the assurance that her family is worried about her, and in all ways must become the general center of attention. The inflated long lower loops, which are at times interlinked with other letters, reflect her materiality and her strong but confused and unrealized sexual desire.

Sample 108. This script of a sixty-year-old business man, written at a period of momentary depression, and therefore containing falling endings, is formed with large movements of the pen, and leftward flourishes. The some-what childish forms lack originality, and mirror the man's hysterical tendencies, while the loops and indolently formed letters, written with a minimum of pressure, substantiate these characteristics. The script contains protective pen movements in the words "vary and getting." The writer wants to patronize the members of his family and attract their attention and admiration, and even carries these drives outside of his family.

Sample 109. The uneven pressure and wide leftward flourishes reveal an exaggeration of emotion and imagination in the handwriting of this thirty-year-old woman. The childish letters indicate the arrested development of a hysterical character, while the dashes and flourishes, unnecessary additions to the letters themselves, symbolize her tendency to turn inwards upon herself. This woman is constantly enthusiastic in her plans for innumerable business ventures, but is easily discouraged, and never accomplishes very much. The unequalness of the small letters discloses her moods which change rapidly from inferiority to those of superiority.

From these different samples, we are able to draw a fairly comprehensive picture of the various feelings of the manifold states of mind which comprise the mysterious and complicated life of the supersensitives.

It is extremely hard to understand a human being. If teachers, parents, and psychologists can understand the mistakes that are made in dealing with the child, and if they do not make the same mistakes themselves, we can be confident that society will come to offer a broader and more understanding scope for all the individual's capacities.

A deeper and wiser comprehension of the different character traits will prevent us from a hasty and superficial judgment. We need to encourage the child at the opportune moment, and, with patience and kindliness must try to overcome the shortcomings and deficiencies of his character. We can all be masters of our actions, taking responsibilities upon our own shoulders. If life is approached in this way, as a cooperative interrelation of independent personalities, we can see no limit to the progress of our human association,

CHAPTER FIFTEEN

MENTAL DISEASES IN HANDWRITING

Today it would be difficult to deny that the individual's mind can influence his actions. If the actions are no more than the mind's tools, we can find ways to develop and improve them. No one, born with a certain standard of intelligence, need remain irredeemably bound to that standard all his life; methods can be found to make the intelligence better equipped to deal with life.

A mind which has lost or misdirected its goal, which is, for instance, undeveloped in an ability to cooperate, will fail to exercise a helpful influence on the growth of the personality. For this reason, we find that many who, as children, lacked cooperativeness, reveal in their maturity a poorly developed intelligence, and a lack of normal social understanding.

Many psychologists have pointed out the consistent relationship between the mind and the body. None of them, however, has attempted to discover the actual bridge between the two.

We must never try to diagnose one symptom, alone, or a single manifestation of abnormality: we must rather study the symptoms in their entirety, and from them discover the underlying fault. In that way we can see the basic error behind the way in which the mind has interpreted its experience, its channeling of life's potentialities, and its reactions to impressions received. This must be the real task of psychology. Psychotic states are not incurable if the neceassary interest in others can be aroused before it is too late; but it places a wider distance between the individual and the normal world than any other condition, except perhaps, the act of committing suicide. It is an intricate

84

art to cure such cases, and an extremely difficult one. We must win the patient back to a cooperative state, and we can only do this through great patience, and the kindest and most understanding manner.

Now let us consider the various mental diseases and the way in which they change the character and behavior of the individual.

Certain types of schizophrenia detach themselves from all outward influences, and lead a wily and self-centered life, attaching importance to nothing but their own poor ego. The neurotic too is mostly concerned with himself, but at times will also take an interest in the life around him. The truly psychotic, however, eventually withdraws completely into himself, becomes indifferent to any external stimulus, and is wholly insensible to everything that happens around, or even to, himself. His egocentricity consists of a detachment from the world, and a resulting and complete isolation.

In comparing the handwriting of the psychotic with those of their earlier and saner lives, we can observe an increased rigidity and monotony, and an impoverishment of forms. The egocentricity of the psychotic does not only manifest itself in involved traits (although fixed and delirious ideas are expressed in involved and futile large backward flourishes), but the increased tendency towards total isolation is mainly mirrored in increasingly static traits and senseless disconnections, which eventually lose any sign of vivacity, speed, or harmoniousness.

Graphic rigidity, therefore, is a symbol of the writer's lack of impressionability, showing him to be insensible to all the variety and rich experiences of the outward world. Just as the mind of the psychotic has no participation in all the fertile influences of this world, their handwriting reflects a similar rigidity and impoverishment of forms. We observe childish letter formation in the handwriting of the educated adult psychotic which revert to the archaic forms of a remote state of civilization. Sample 113.

In the following handwritings we shall see graphic

reflections of the mentally diseased who isolate themselves from the world and live in a confused, fictitious life.

Dementia praecox or schizophrenia is the collective term for the three manifestations of the diseased mind: hebephrenia, catatonia, and paranoia.

The latter is a mental disease in which delusions of grandeur and especially persecution play a dominent part. The individual feels that everyone, or one particular person at least, is set against him. Not only does he suspect that the world is antagonistic towards him, but he also believes that everyone is actually planning to harm, or even destroy, him.

A paranoiac condition may either develop gradually and imperceptibly from early life, or may appear without warning in maturity, usually, but not always, as a consequence of some critical occurrence in the individual's life. Becoming suspicious of what he believes to be evil intentions of those around him, he withdraws more and more from society, until he has completely retreated into his own delusions.

While the paranoiac's mind is lost in the labyrinth of one particular delusion, his faculties, except when they touch his special delusion, remain quite normal. A paranoiac may be obsessed with fixed and unwarranted suspicions about his business partner, for instance, and may yet be most logical and perceptive in all other respects. His memory is, as a rule, normal, his perception acute, and his judgment clear and rational; it is only when his attention is directed towards his partner that he becomes irrational and abnormal. Paranoiacs usually develop some from of defense against their imagined persecutors. They may heap insults and violent reproaches upon an innocent and very surprised neighbor, and even injure him physically, as well. At times the paranoiacs who suspect the world at large, and respond aggressively to these suspicions, become very dangerous.

Sample 110. This handwriting illustrates clearly the fixed idea of persecution; this man draws unconsciously the portrait of his business partner on an envelope addressed to the person in question.

86

Among paranoiacs we find quarrelsome people, so inflexible in all their opinions that they are always ready to nag and argue at the slightest sign of disagreement.

Sample 111. This script uncovers another case of paranoia. Since early childhood, this man has showed all the characteristics of the paranoiac nature; he was reserved, did not make friends with his school mates, and was totally uncooperative.

Though he is of only average intelligence, he succeeded in his business career through his great and pedantic sense of duty. He has always had a supersensitive memory. His affection for his family, while genuine, was almost suspicious, and his distrust is mirrored in his very narrow angle, In sample 112, we again see this writer's script, but we must notice how his unfavorable paranoiac disposition has developed into insanity. The angle, and in fact the whole writing, becomes more narrow, and is nearly squeezed together into unbroken lines of connected words, illustrating the severe delusions of persecution and his constant hallucinations. It is easy to see that his mind has become totally disrupted. He has now been in an asylum for many years without any sign of improvement.

Often delusions of grandeur rather than of persecution fill the mind of the paranoiac. He sees himself as an unquestionably distinguished personage. Just as the paranoiac suffering from delusions of persecution sees the world bent on his destruction, so the other, obsessed by his imaginary grandeur, deludedly realizes that he is revered and exalted in the eyes of the world. Paranoia, in fact, may manifest itself in an endless variety and confirmation of delusions.

Sample 113. This script reveals the delusions of grandeur in a woman of paranoiac disposition, who is a gifted painter. She always thought and behaved in a fantastic manner, and was unable to make any statement without confounding the facts with her own imaginings. She was never aware that she was even practicing any deception. She was also hysteric: protesting her great sympathy and

87

tender-heartedness to everyone who would listen, while, in reality, she was totally self-centered. She was never able to cooperate, detaching herself from all responsibilities. She had the fixed idea that her mission in life is to redeem the world. Though gifted as an artist, she lacked creative imagination and discipline, and was unable to concentrate her thoughts on her work.

The handwriting shows a disorder in which the formation of the letters is unclear. Her egocentricity and distorted attitude are reflected in the loose, pressureless, and occasionally dramatically flourished letters.

While, in paranoia the patient accuses all mankind, in melancholia he accuses himself alone, and suffers intensely from inordinate and fantastic self-reproaches. Melancholia is one of the mental disorders which are a great trial to all the people with whom the sufferer comes in contact. Melancholics are often inclined to punish themselves by committing suicide, and must be closely watched at all times. In order to treat them conscientiously, the attending physician must be an especially well-trained psychologist, never contradicting them or letting them realize that he has made them change their minds, or, in fact, doing anything to arouse their aggressive self-castigation.

Sample 114. This handwriting reveals a severe case of melancholia. The slow, hesitant, and rigid words and letters written with uneven and smeary pressure, reflect a deep state of depression. This woman will remain silent for weeks and even months, remaining frozen in a cataleptic state, unconscious of the passage of time, or even of her discomfort. The anxiety and fear which tormented her eventually drove her to attempt suicide. When she was frustrated she immediately made a second and equally unsuccessful attempt.

The entire psychological make-up and deterioration of the maniac, (the insane person in the active period of manic-depression) as well as his writing characteristics, are entirely different from the preceding types. His expressions are

88

lively and changeable caricatures of the faces he sees around him, his eyes dart about, and his movements are sudden and full of amazing energy. The maniac's whole drive is towards activity, he is restless and obstreperous, and indefatigable.

Sample 115. In the handwriting of this educated and well-bred man, we see delusions of grandeur which are due to a maniac excitement. The ascending lines show that his optimism is at its height; enclosed in his dream world, he cannot conceive of the failure of any of his plans. Wide flourishes and dashing movements of the pen show the vivid flow of his abstruse ideas and extravagant imagination. A suddenly increasing pressure on single strokes discloses his excitement and excess of emotion. When he wrote this, he was in the highest period of his elation.

Sample 116. This is written by the same person, but in a depressive period, and in a somewhat more lucid state of mind, which took place some months before the maniac attack. In comparing these two samples, we notice how the writing traits of the depressive period are enlarged in the maniac state, and follow an accentuation parallel to that taken by the course of his disease.

Logical thinking among the psychotic is common rather than rare. But the logical faculty of a psychotic person is usually of only slight advantage to him, for either his reasons are based on a false premise, or should they be correct, betray his insane condition when he attempts to apply his logic to a given situation.

The great split between the internal and external worlds between self and environment is observed in schizophrenia. In this disease, a weakening and distortion of the emotional life and the will-power take place long before the intellect is affected. We notice a strange change of character, lack of attention and cooperation, such weariness that work is impossible, and sudden extreme impulses which alternate with indolence.

In the progression of this malady, there may be a com-

89

plete disinterest in the external world. There are schizophrenics who live for years in a hospital without expressing the least wish to see their relatives and friends, and do not even pay any attention to the doctors and other patients. In the advanced stages of this disease-dementia praecox-there is almost no hope of curing the patient. The name of the disease itself means a pronounced and hopeless mental decay.

In schizophrenia we often find delusions of grandeur and persecution, as well as erotic delirium. The fantasies of the schizophrenics, however, are not as systematically constructed as those of paranoiacs, but are less coherent, and filled with absurd contradictions.

Sample 117. This script shows a grave case of schizophrenia in an advanced stage of the disease-that is to say, dementia praecox. This woman was a gifted writer, and a student of the fine arts. Even in her early childhood, she was asocial, isolating herself from companions, and showing strongly pessimistic tendencies. Her handwriting covers the page like a cobweb, without any realization that there should be spacing between words and lines. As the flourishes encircle her words, her egocentric thoughts surround only herself. We see, through the uniquely formed letters, the evidence of her trained and able mind, which however, is, at this point, completely lacking in any ability to reason.

Sample 119. This is the handwriting of a scientist who is afflicted with dementia praecox. This man is now obsessed with a religious delirium, after having passed through a catatonic period. He continually prays for redemption from sins which he believes he has committed, assuming most uncomfortable and distorted positions, or sometimes kneeling for hours and even days. He is not aware of what happens around him, and, as is typical of the cataleptic, has no realization that questions are being asked, or food offered. His handwriting is completely unbalanced, bending to all sides like reeds shaken in the wind. His obsession is clearly symbolized in the small flower-like design in the margin opposite the fifth line. This sort of pattern is frequently used by the catatonic, symbolizing his encircled thoughts with its concentric circles.

Sample 118. This sample was written by a woman afflicted with syphilitic hallucinations. Some graceful and independent letter formations reveal her educated and well-trained mind. This writer possesses artistic ability, and was at one time a gifted writer. Her imagination, however, was always extravagant and incoherent.

Her writing shows many uncertain and trembling strokes, and undulating lines. Her uncertain coordination, and her inability to descend stairs safely, or even to walk success-fully are reflected in her awkward handling of the pen. She displays difficulties in articulation, and her handwriting mirrors this defect in the jerky fashion with which she puts the words on paper.

This writing took place in a period of great mental excitement; her elation and even violence, is disclosed in the heavy horizontal strokes. She is in very high spirits, at this point, and is most obstreperous, displaying no signs of fatigue. At its beginning, this script appears to be quite orderly, but little by little it becomes hurried, growing larger in its impatience, showing the writer's confusion and absurd thoughts and impulses. She is talkative, and her mind cannot produce any logical thoughts.

There are three states of mania: mild, acute, and delir-ious mania, the latter being clearly described in Sample 118. It is incorrect to believe that the individual who suffers from a mild mania is necessarily abnormal. The peculiarities which the sufferer develops are not sufficiently pronounced to cause him to be classified as psychotic, or even unbalanced. His rational powers do not deteriorate: his comprehension, his reason, his judgment show no signs of impairment. In fact, his perception and attention show an increased alert-ness, and his temperament gains in vivaciousness. But this individual correspondingly develops a certain fickleness which he displays in all his actions as well as in all his relationships. Even the most resolute and serious individual, when attacked by this neurosis, undergoes a complete transformation of his awareness. His seriousness gradually vanishes, and is supplanted by a certain degree of mutability. His ideas are no longer centered on one major goal, and his activities become decentralized, although not necessarily disorganized. His interests in life, too, undergo a metamorphosis. Some things which he formerly regarded with indifference or even contempt, now become objects of serious concern, and to them he devotes a great deal of his time.

Sample 120. This is the handwriting of a woman who is still active in the business world, although her changing moods and excitability make it hard for her associates to get on with her. She displays an intense craving for activity; however, this is not the activity of a person who is stimulated by a definite drive, but rather that which is instigated by an inner restlessness. Although the writing discloses a marked indolence revealed by the slowness of tempo, in this state she became exceedingly active. For instance, she writes many letters, often sending an unusual number to one person at short intervals, constantly repeating the same phrases, or even duplicating the previous letters in their entirety. She became excessively impatient in her business dealings, feeling that her projects are progressing much too slowly.

In order to preserve peace, one should agree with this maniac type as much as is possible, for any disagreement arouses their irritability, and provokes an avalanche of protests. We meet this type almost daily, and it is important to realize that his difficult attitude stems from a neurotic disturbance, if one is to deal successfully with him.

The patient usually passes from simple to acute mania if treated mistakenly. Here, the tendency to indulge in excessive activity does not subside in the least, but the actions show an increasing lack of concentration and control. The individual may become actively destructive, even breaking furniture as a release.

The next stage into which he may pass is called delirious mania, of which sample 119 was an example. The victim loses here complete control over his thoughts, and hallucinations become more and more frequent, so that communication with the patient is, at this stage, practically impossible. The writer of sample 119 suffers from auditory hallucinations, and hears what he claims to be the voice of God. Such symptoms as this are continuously heard, starting in the early stages of the disease and continuing to the end.

There can be no doubt that the delusions of the insane would prove to have some meaning, if only we knew how to translate them. Clinical psychiatry troubles itself little about the actual form of the individual symptoms or the content of it. We cannot deny that the symptom itself has a meaning and is connected with experiences in the life of the patient.

The analysis of handwriting can be an invaluable clue if applied in a direction which we have tried to give with our examples. We can only assert, we cannot prove that it is so in every case. Graphology is a young science, and time and application will open a way for a better understanding of the delusions which torture the mind of the insane.

CONCLUSION

This study has been an attempt at clarifying the irrefutable connection between an individual's handwriting, its development and idiosyncrasies, and his personality, - whether it changes from normal to neurotic, or insane, or whether it develops a more constant pattern.

As has been pointed out, the handwriting is a key to the often obscure and latent potentialities of the child; it is an infallible graph by which the parents, teachers, and especially the psychologist can chart the course of the child's emotional and intellectual growth, and see into a future full of promise or destruction. Naturally, the script alone is not sufficient to reveal every eventual triumph or misstep; the child's enviroment, his reactions and habits must also be taken into account. Graphology, obviously, is not a

93

black science, and one should be warned against the staggering boasts of the charlatan graphologist. On the other hand, this science is a most important factor in planning the child's life, in deciding on the course of his education, and the stringency of his discipline; it should be used as a visual case history, to be referred to from time to time as a check on the affirmative growth of his personality.

In the case of the neurotic or insane, the individual's script over a period of years can become psychological milestones, by which the physician can trace his way back to the earliest and most incipient manifestations of the disease in question. As has been demonstrated repeatedly, there is an unshakable parallel between the individual's sane and insane characteristics, and his writing throughout each period. The pen becomes a direct expression of the patient's disease. Each letter, each flourish, every sign of speed or hesitancy, is a substantiation of the individual's intangible obsessions and uncertainties, until the written page becomes a montage of his peculiar neurosis, or of his unmistakable genius.

Havana. 27th June 1939

this is a specimen of my
handwriting—
I am 26 years old. Male.— **1**

July 21, 1939 **2**

Dear Mme Marcuse,

I am seventeen years
old of a masculine sex. I am

3

Madame Irene Marcuse
My age is 47 Sex Male
I have read your ads
Sunday Times. I would like
Tr... ... - ... ...
Havana Post. **4**

Dear Madame, I am
a woman, born 1903. 17th of Dec

95

Irene Marcuse
presso Dose [illegible]
Via Cairoli 48 Città 5

my handwriting, for which I
I am enclosing herewith my 6
[illegible]

like you to give a reading of it
and don't hesitate to tell the bad. 7
Thank you in anticipation
yours truly
[illegible]

Nom de Plume

Dear Madam Marcuse,
Having followed your
column in [illegible]
[illegible]
would be the first [illegible], I'll be in
anxious, if I am going to be [illegible] 9
the [illegible]. [illegible]
on me
[illegible] and [illegible]

11 did not feel me for an apology... there
do you feel better?
All here Past. & S. . . . .

12
Mme Irene Marcuse
% The Havana Post

13 Dear Mme. Marcuse:
As a constant reader of
The Havana Post, I shall

14 apologize for not having written to you before and
thanked you for your very kind letter of congratulation.

Para ver su opinion sobre
15 la mia. ~

16 he should be so happy if some
day you would come to

17 surprised, I think. Though I
usually can — in your case,

very much like to see you,
and now that our finances

To write you
everything just
Apr. 1947.
[signature]

Madame Marcuse,
of The Habana Post,
Industria 165

Habana. **19**

20

Mrs Irene Marcuse
243 West 100 St
New York City 25; N.Y.

were Returned to you **21**
in two books — and send
at the volume $5.00
Saturday April 27th —

98

22

December 28th 193[illegible]

Dear Mrs Marcuse.-

I wonder just what my hand-writing reveals to you. Won't you please tell me.

I hope not giving you my name won't matter but I am female and around the middle thirties.

23

[illegible] e augurio tutte e buone cose dell' Esposizione, intanto [illegible] to con affetto —

Vittoria

§ 24

24

Ich [illegible] Ihnen den Brief mit vielem Dank zurück. Ich bin mit meinen Nachforschungen bezüglich des Themas noch nicht zu Ende, [illegible] oder gelegentlich über das Thema sprechen. — Morgen gehe ich [illegible] und bin Montag wieder hier. Montag [illegible]

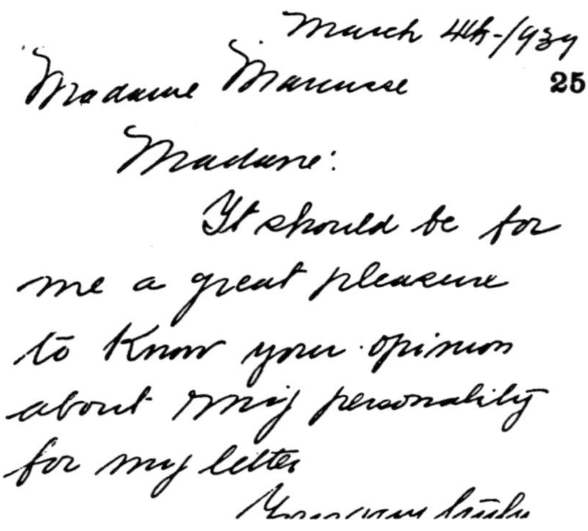

March 4th/1939

Madame Marcuse   25

   Madame:

     It should be for me a great pleasure to know your opinion about my personality for my letter

       [signature illegible]

junior million
I am a boy   26
age 11

Punctuation marks are signals or symbols which a writer uses to make clear to the reader what he means. If you occasionally receive unpunctuated, uncapitalized letters, you know that they and that sometimes the meaning isn't clear. Such a letter is usually uninteresting. The reader is impressed only by the mistakes,

100

Arthur J. Hammel   Age - 12   Sex - By

Thither, midst falling dew
While glow the heavens with the last steps of day
Far, through their rosy depths, dost thou pursue
Thy solitary way?

Vainly the foster's eye
Might mark thy distant flight to do thee wrong.
As, darkly painted on the crimson sky
Thy figure floats along.

Carolie Roundy   :28
age: 12
sex: girl

Quality of Mercy.
                    William Shakespeare
The Quality of Mercy is not strained,
It droppeth as the gentle rain,

Name.   Wm Jay Malone   29
Age.   twelve years old.
Sex.   masculine

            Opportunity

Master of human destiny am I.
Fame, love, and fortune on my footsteps waits,
Cities and fields I walk, I penetrate

30 Medora Webster

girl

Age 13

Punctuation marks are signals or symbols
which a writer uses to make clear to the reader
what he means. If you occasionally receive
unpunctuated, uncapitalized letters, you know
that they are hard to read and that sometimes
the meaning isn't clear. Such a letter is
usually uninteresting. The reader is impressed
only by the mistakes.

31   'William Allen (boy)   Age - 12   31

Punctuation marks are signals or symbols which a
writer uses to make clear to the reader what he means
If you occasionally receive unpunctuated, uncapitalized
letters, you know that they are hard to read and that
sometimes the meaning isn't clear. Such a letter is usually
uninteresting. The reader is impressed only by the mistakes

The End

32 Edyth Alice Holl (girl)   grade. 1.   Age 12   32

———More than three hundred years ago, a band
of refugees landed on the rocky coast of New England
They were men, women and children who wanted to
worship God acordingly to the dictates of their own
consciences.

Just three hundred nineteen years ago they
started the Plymouth colony in Massachusetts.

Age 12

Frank Preston (boy)

Punctuation marks are signals or symbols which a writer uses to make clear to the reader what he means. If you occasionally receive unpunctuated, uncapitalized letters, you know that they are hard to read and that sometimes the meaning isn't clear. Such a letter is usually uninteresting. The reader is impressed only by the mistakes.

Richard E. Robinson
I am a boy
Age 11

34

Dear Mr. Ruton,
Punctuation marks are signals or symbols which a writer uses to make clear to the reader what he means. If you recieve unpunctuated, uncapitalized letters, you know that they are hard to read and that sometimes the meaning isn't clear. Such a letter is usually uninteresting. The reader is impressed only by the mistakes.

Dear Mrs. Marcuse,

I am a girl, almost seventeen years old. I would like to know if my hand-writing reveals talent in acting, clothes-modelling, or writing. I will be anxiously awaiting my answer, and I hope that other things will also be revealed.

Thank you
"Priscilla"

The Editor

Havana Post. Apt. 989   36

Havana, Cuba

Dear Mme. Marcuse,

    I am sending in a sample
of my handwriting. Will you please
analyze it for me?

    I am a girl of thirteen
and in first year high school. I
live in Cuba, but was born
in the United States.

    Inclosed you will find
twenty cents in stamps. If my
answer appears in the Havana
Post, please call me "number 13."
Thank you very much.

            Yours truly,

            Phyllis Kloote

Dear Miss Day,

    dont think I forgot
about you. I love you
just as much as I
used to, in fact even
more Perhaps you would
like to hear about self
I am in the forth grade
now. Yesterday we received
letters from the children

close now got its time
to go to bed
give my love to miss
Long. And Sheilah
sends her love to you.
    Your very old pupil
    Elaine Brody

38

12 years old

Elaine Brady   June 10, 1930
        History

1. A labor union is an organization of working men in the same line of work trying to better their working condition

2. A strike was the putting of work by union men in a body to secure better working conditions, higher wages, or shorter hours.

3. A Boycott is the refusal to deal with an employer while the employees are on strike

4. Sabotage is the willful destruction of machinery in a factory by the employees while there is labor trouble. This forces the employer to meet their terms

5. Picketing is the watching or guarding of a factory by union men, to prevent non-union men from taking their place and helping the employer.

107

be her fate? Was she never to see her people again? Carol Launcher's heart beat fast as these dreadful thoughts flashed through her mind. In another second they were no longer thoughts, and Carol Launcher finding herself trapped by her enemies threw herself in path of the horses — wishing rather to be trampled to death, than branded a prisoner and burned at the stake. The young Minnetaree chief who was in the lead, ordered his men carefully around the girl and ordered her taken and bound. Somewhere on Carol Launcher is on a quest — a quest for happiness with her people, the Sioux.

This book is very interestingly told — not in first person but in third. It is a real story — full of excitement, mystery, adventure and all the attributes which make a fine book. The characters are not ordinary, but they are definite individuals each having a singular characteristics. It is which I would highly recommend to anyone as an enjoyable biography.

Dear Miss Hampton,

I don't know Richard's address. Would you be so kind as to notify him of the contents of my note? I'd appreciate it greatly.

How is your mother? Please give her my regards.

Thank you so much.

Elaine Brody

April 28.

18 years old

"Mike Adams is my name. seventeen million young men are
have a been registered under the selective serve act at the
same time, young men and women are being instructed to
pilot airplanes.

Mike Adams
179 Norfolk St.
New York, N.Y.

41

(12 y 60 wold)
42

42 Stanley Adams is my or name
it Seventeen millian young man
have been registered under the
selective setrice oct at the
same time young men and women
are to being instructed to pilot
airplanes

Stanley adams
179 Narbolk St
New York N.Y.

1 10

(10 y 00 wole)

IV

43 Female - aged 50 years.

Will my health improve during this year, 1939, and what will be best for me - rest and quiet or activities? Will business be better for me this year and shall I continue to remain in Cuba?

I have been told that my lucky number is 5 - but I believe 28 is luckier for me.

44 This is the yuletide season, when men of good will should rejoice.

45 I am mostly at home - teaching a lot, and if you want to

111

Havana,
23 Nov. 1939

The Editor
Havana Post

att: Mme Marcuse

From the standpoint
of curiosity I herewith
submit this specimen of

S. 47'

april 4th

age 56
Female

Dear madam Marcuse
please send and tell me
what my handwriting reveal
Heather

Habana, February 22ⁿᵈ, 1939

Dear Mrs. Marcuse,

Would greatly appreciate your
analyzing my handwriting.

My trouble is that I feel depressed
and unhappy most of the time without
particular reason. Would you say that I am
a sick man or just overworked and in need

Liebe Freundin, Da ich Ihre neue
Adresse nicht kannte, habe ich
Ihnen nach der alten geschrieben.
Haben Sie erhalten? Mich sehr
mit Ihrer Nachricht gefreut.
Wir sind hier am äussersten Ende
Amerikas! nahe San Diego.
Der Sohn ist in Los Angeles. Wir
wollten ihn in seiner Nähe sein.
Sie sehen also auch nicht den Ocean.
Nächste Frühjahr kommen in jedem Fall
nach Europa & hoffen Sie dann zu
sehen. Herzl. Grüsse Ihr Friedberg

113

"Dear Mrs. Marcuse –

I am enclosing twenty cents in stamps as directed, in the hope of seeing my handwriting analyzed in the Havana Post within a day or two.

51

July 23rd

Dear Harriet

Your escapade of two nights ago, in spite of my warning to you about that bunch, I find it impossible to take as a matter of course. I have decided to end our engagement.

114

"Johnny"

Sixteen decrees have been
published for the increase
and priority in production
of goods for the national
defense. They call for
economies through the sup-
pression of financial
autonomy in 15 govern-
mental organizations to

"Hilda"

For his part, Senator Zin has
been able to make considerable capital
out of the charge that the Growers
Union is chainstore inspired and
chain-store operated and has much
less interest in the po' farmer than
the growers claim the Senator has
          The net of the thing is that
the farmer will probably go to the
group which he, at the moment,
thinks will give him the better deal.
At present it looks as if the Growers

S 54   Farmer   Havana Cuba   54
                   March 26-1939

Madame Marcuse
     I am a male age 47.
Reading your daily hand writing
in the post. I thought I also
might send you a few lines. as I
am sure you will be able to tell
me something about my health

55   Madame Marcuse   Sex. female   55
                  Seeing your advertisemet
about analyzing hand writing I would like
to know what mine signifies and how
is my physical condition.
            Yours 266.
signed
eight hundred sixty eight.   56
    (18.5.1868)
       I am a man

          I remain
         Dear Madam
            Your Obedient Servant
               Hartwig Henry

J. 5.7)   July 31, 1939

57

Joe dear,

I received your letter. I was beginning to think it would never get here. To day is a lovely day we are ...... to the beach. It rained all

58   Mme Irene Marcus   58

Habana

Estimada Señora:

Con gran interés he leído sus trabajos en el Havana Post y le acompaño $0.40 su sello me los dos anal...

59   Dear Madam:-   59

I am thirtysix years old, male
Would like to know your
Character analysed of my hand writing.
Thanking you, I remain.
Yours very truly

117

somehow you could assist me.
I am twenty six years of age – masculine sex.
Could you tell me why I am so unlucky in everything.
What can I do to make my dreams come true? I

62. For many

44 yrs of age. Am also enclosing **61**
another sample for analysis to
see what you have to say about
it. Your articles are very interesting and I hope my reading
will be favorable.

Thanking you in advance

62   Irene Mosmoc.   **62**

Dear Madam:

I am thirty five years of age and of the

masculine gender.

Yours very truly.
Gallito

S. 43   63

Mr. Marcuse;
        As two of our professors
were going to drive to Viñales
this afternoon, they invited
Mr. Ruston and was quite
anxious that he go. The

63 Dear Madame —   64

    Will you please
send in mail the
analization of my
writing —
        California
Enclosed 40 in stamps
+ extra stamps for mail

S. 45

Dear Madam Marcuse: 65

        Will you please send
in your very interesting way, the enclosed
specimen of handwriting, identified as
follow:

119

Madame,

I am writing these lines in the hope that you will do as you have in many other similar cases, namely, analyze the handwriting.

Requirements are age & sex. I am male & 30 years old.

66 May I send you specimen lines for your courtesy?

67 Dear Madam: 67

Would you mind making an analysis of my handwriting, stating frankly what you find, whether favorable, or unfavorable?

Am enclosing your usual fee of twenty cents in postage stamps.

Sincerely yours,

68 from my handwriting, of which this is a specimen — Herewith 20¢ in postage stamps to cover your fee —

Very truly
Preston Holmes.

120

69

70 There is nothing worrying me but I would like to have you analyze my hand-writing

70

71

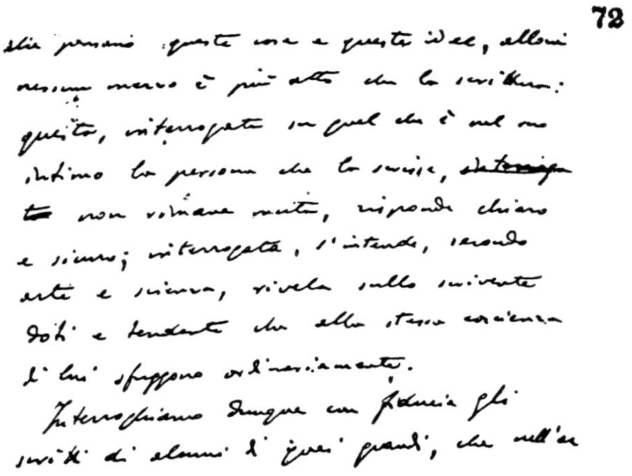

72

stia pensando queste cose e queste idee, allora nessun mezzo è più atto che la scrittura: questa, interrogata in quel che è nel suo intimo la persona che la scrive, ~~interrogata~~ non rimane muta, risponde chiaro e sicuro; interrogata, s'intende, secondo arte e scienza, rivela sullo scrivente doti e tendenze che alla stessa coscienza di lui sfuggono ordinariamente.

Interroghiamo dunque con fiducia gli scritti di alcuni di genii grandi, che nell'ar

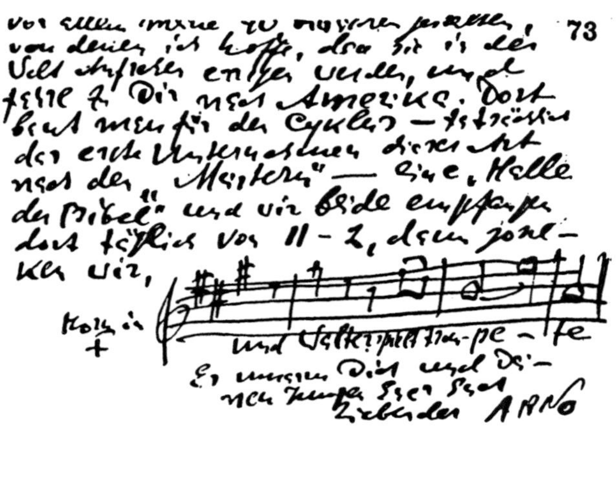

73

vor allem immer zu wünschen gestatten, von denen ich hoffe, dass sie in der Welt Aufsehen erregen werden, und fahre zu Dir nach Amerika. Dort baut man für den Cyklus — hoffentlich das erste Unternehmen dieser Art nach den „Mysterien" — eine „Halle der Bibel" und wir beide empfangen dort täglich von 11 – 2, denn jodel- ken wir,

Es umarmen Dich und Dei- nen Jungen
Dich Liebender ARNO

74' 3 What did the ranchman said when he saw
Waht, "That! If that was Waht that he never 74
saw a bear in her life like Waht! Why that is
the worst grizzly that ever rolled a log in the
Big Horn Basin."

75   hay ⊥ 11   **75**
As you can see, on the farms and in the
villages and towns and small cities 9
great many of our people live in one-
family or two family houses with
lawns and gardens and places for play
around them

76   Ich hatte 3 Monate Ferien und jetzt weiss ich
wieder fleissig in die Schule gehen. Haben einen jungen
Lehrer bekommen, der mich sehr an Sie erinnert. Es hat
in Oxford "Barrister" studiert. — Mein Vater lernt auch
fleissig English.   **76**
    Nun zu Ihnen: Wir sind sehr neugierig zu

So hairdressing a
way out from this tiring
job of child caring — I'd
like to be myself for
a few years before I

            77:

Nov. 12, 1939   **78**

Dear Mrs. Marcuse,

Enclosed you'll find a sample of a script I'd like you to analyze us to the following:

Is this man (49 years) to be trust and do you think it advisable for a woman to contract a marriage with him.

J.81

J.79

February 22, 1939   **79**

My dear Mme. Marcuse —

I would like to know why I Can't make up my mind about important things and why I care so much about what people will say if I make ____

J.80

Havana, Cuba.
March 8-1939.

80

Dear Madam Marcuse :—
I have read with great interest your different analyses of handwriting in N. Havana Post. I have enjoyed your lecture at the Woman's Club.

(margin, right side, vertical) J.81 The handwriting people are of my species. Life's work — a battling pact

124

82

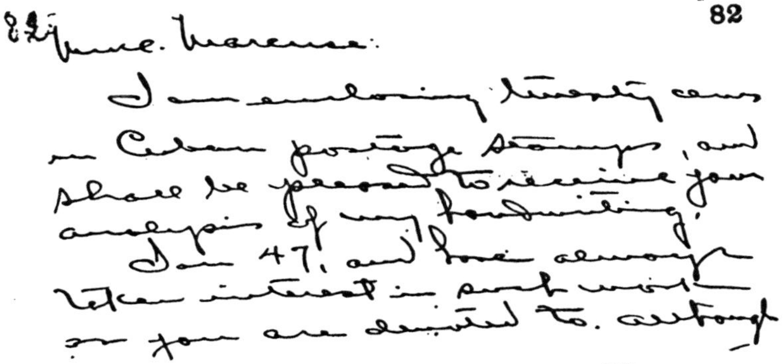

Mme. Marcuse:
I am enclosing twenty cents in Cuban postage stamps, and shall be pleased to receive your analysis of my handwriting.
I am 47, and have always taken interest in such work as you are devoted to. Although

83

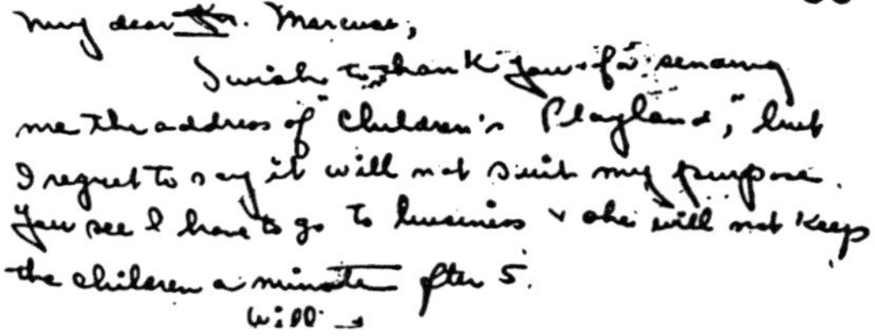

My dear Dr. Marcuse,
I wish to thank you for sending me the address of "Children's Playland," but I regret to say it will not suit my purpose. You see I have to go to business & she will not keep the children a minute after 5.
6:00

84

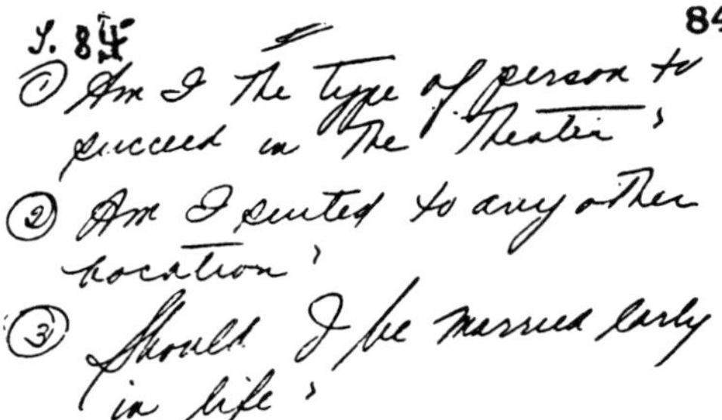

S. 84
(1) Am I the type of person to succeed in the Theater?
(2) Am I suited to any other vocation?
(3) Should I be married early in life?
(4) What type of person would

Essere e parere.

Le persone non sono ridicole se non quando vogliono parere od essere ciò che non sono.

Il povero, gli ignoranti, il rustico, il malato, il vecchio non sono mai ridicoli, mentre si contentano di parer tali, essi tengono nei meriti voluti da queste loro qualità; massi bene quando il vecchio vuol parer giovane, il malato sano il povero ricco, l'ignorante vuol fare dell' istrutto il rustico del cittadino.

... ...

bei meinem Hiersein sehr gute Dienste gelei-
stet hat. Das Wetter ist hier ganz herrlich, zwar
hatten wir heute ein starkes Gewitter mit einem
Niederschlägen, aber trotzdem sind wir froh, wun-
ter und alles in allem gute Laune.
Wie geht es Ihnen und Ihren Lieben, wa-

86

... ... unter dem allerdings Medina sich als
... ... als Mekka. Ich habe
eben ... ... der dumpfe Widerstand ... Ihren
Pläne ... ... der deutlich gezeigt, so eindeutig pe-
... ... sein Ursprung war — ich habe ... diesem

87

88.

Sogni mere ... il desiderio
d'ottenere ... ... una
réalité nere il ... ...
les cour ... ... Selez
Vita
es allora ... ...
che ... — una ... una
... di ... ...

88

I.

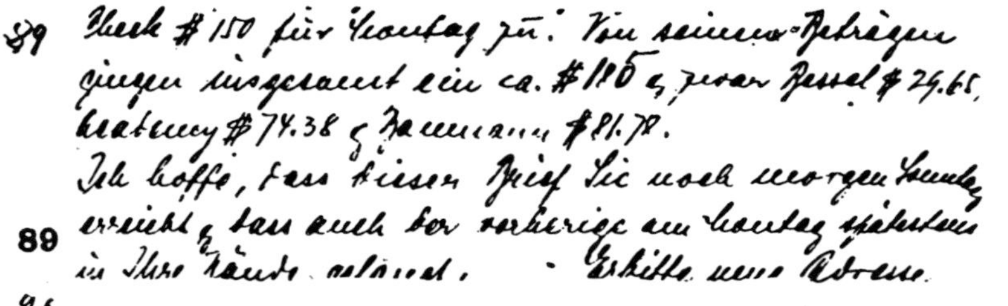

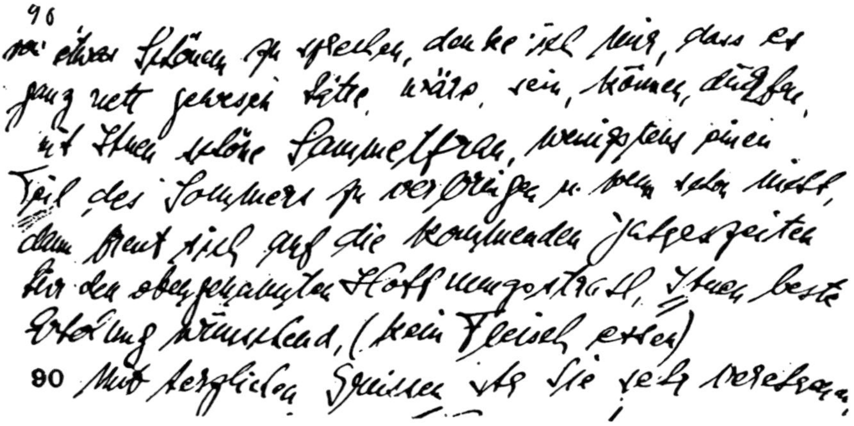

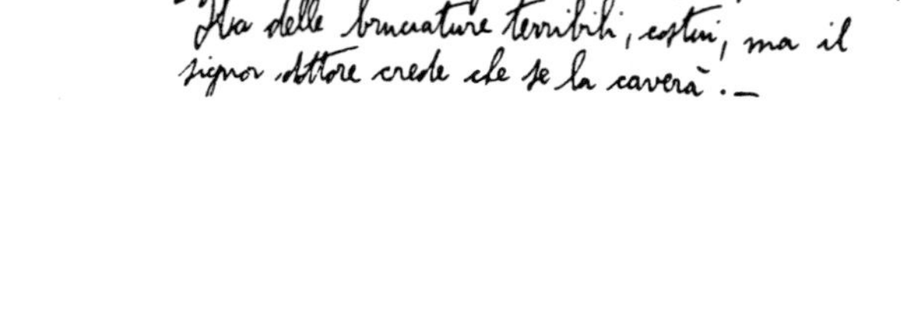

Colonel whose principal dut
exactly where groups of hot
he became the most famo
He received the familiar n
the great service he rendered
railroad was built between,
This railroad was constructe
gold in California. One seri
wants supply food for the
The government offered to
which were used for meat
Colonel Cody started out
killed more buffaloes than
that time Colonel Cody was

... la [ill_] ... ...
Kommen, bringt etwas mit. ...
sind mich freuen, ... und Ihren
Sohn am Sonnabend abend (morgen)
zwischen 20.30 und 21.00 Uhr ...
begrüßen zu kommen
          Beste Grüße
          [signature]

Sunday afternoon I went out with aunt Else. We had tea together and afterwards went to the movie: Queen Christine! It was lovely.

Rondello had invited me for supper. There was also Dr. Ricco and his wife and a young boy, whose name I forgot. It was very nice and Dr. Ricco sends kind regards.

Wednesday uncel Oscar invited me for lunch and in the evening I am invited to Dr. Ricco, also Rondello and that boy.

Qui si riceverà del materiale e sarà lieto per la
mia tesi; ricerca un po' inquieta dette le scienze,
non solo pubblicazioni televisive e pur seri che ancora
le mia conoscenza del tedesco è un po' arretrate.
Per un mio fermento e credere di fare del mio
meglio. Altro novità non vi sarebbero, ormai non
mi pare opportuno communicartele per lettera. Io
le dirò a voce quanto ormai quaggiù.
Le nostro comuni amiche domandano molto
spesso di te e con una certa ironia tutta quelle,
ma io, come al solito, sono ammi riservato. 95

96

both ideas expressed, also that I am
mean and hard - while others say I am
too kind hearted and only hard on me
Don't judge my education by my
handwriting - people say I'm intellect
but I just never could write,.
Thanking you ... for any information
you may give me, I am,
96 very sincerely,.

131

Rye new york. and I have been in
cuba for nearly two years.
I now hope to be able to go to
new york and get into some kind **97**
of work.

Dear Madam

I read a piece in the
Hanava post about you. I would
lo know what you can do for
me. I am a jamaican I was born
in the year 1880 in the moth of
2-6 February. I am 5-9 years old
I am in bad luck cannot keep **98**
... ..
.6, 1896.
I shall appreciate your remarks
thru the columns of Havana Post in respect
of my immediate and future personal and
business problems.
Ten 3 ct. cuban postage stamps are
enclosed herewith.
Thanking you in advance, I remain,
Very truly yours, **99**
G O C

S. 100. Fortunately it was
my right lens which
broke and it is
very inexpensive,
the left one is the one
made to a special perscription

S. 101
Compadécete de tu madre.
Compadécete de tu padre
Compadécete de tus hermanos
Compadécete de ti.
Cosa triste es el hombre

102

Almería, den 5 Juli 1934

Sehr geehrte Frau ...

... Folge ... und in die ...
und ... Festen ...

133

S 103- feb 4th 41 103

Dear Ruth
Just a line to
tell you I realy
enjoyed my self

[illegible]

Hiefe gearbeitet. [illegible] sollen
Wie geht's: Dir's Walter? [illegible] Brief
[illegible] Dir dort ein Brief
[illegible] Trotz aller Sorgen [illegible] in Paris
[illegible]. Trotz [illegible] Kann das man
doch immer noch am besten. [illegible] Revolution
ein neues Land [illegible] dort Revolution

[illegible] Dir recht gut [illegible] vielleicht [illegible]
sogar [illegible], was ich Dir jetzt im Sommer
wünsche. Alles Gute von Herzen 104
[illegible]

Dr. [illegible]

105

S. 107 July 6th 1939

Dear Mme Marcuse 105

I am indeed
interested in your analyses. I am
a woman my age is 54 years old
I would like you to search out
my character clear. Waiting your
reply.

80'6 Милый и дорогой Арвед! Сегодня получила от
одной рисанки письмо в котором она меня передает то,
что прочла в картах, брошенных для меня. Я очень
спешила сегодня и не вникла еще [в] то, что оно в
нем излагала, но одно мне ясно что ты сам мне —
ский самый хороший человек в мире и меня очень
любишь. Скажи мой Арвед, милый и любимый, при-
едешь ли ты. Я хочу, чтобы ты непременно
приехал, я буду очень, очень рада и счастлива Пус[ть]
любимка поможет устроить твою поездку сюда.
Мы будем бродить целыми днями в городе а затем
доём, его удивлял некоторые поездки ь и в дру-
гие города насколько нам позволят это наши де-
нежные условия. Увидишь, как будет прекрасн[о]
а

June 13, 1939
Havana, Cuba

f. 104

Mme. Marcuse
% Havana Post
Dear Mme. Marcuse,
Will you kindly tell me what you can of my abilities, talents (if any?)
faults — or what have you? What
qualities do I possess as a wife,
mother, friend? What indications
do you see of a financial or business
head? Do you always discount a

108 My dear Mrs. Marcuse,

I enjoyed your letter very much & thank God I am feeling now much improved. Tho I still have pains & impediments in locomotion of my right thigh, I am on my way to recovery & am busy in my office daily. Glad to learn that you are getting

---

109

August 25, 1935

Mme. Marcuse,
The Mariana Post,
Parana.

Dear Madam
I am enclosing herewith 2d in stamps

110

Erson

111

Lario il mio collegio il Mr Signor Capo di Stato curio lte riceuta da cordialita, guar dando a quelle de inuia furono licon- eguente non poso faca meno di dire

J. 114

me come un appoggio perchè la distanza è troppo grande; penso sempre che attribuisce alla malattia delle parole che mi detta il buon senso – Dunque desidero e chiamo con tutta la forza del mio essere la prigione; perchè il delitto non è ripugnante come la pazzia e l'imbecillità – Forse i guerrieri slavi miei antenati i quali tagliavano le teste, bruciavano i villaggi e passavano in un turbine di sangue e di delitti, forse non erano pazzi e credevano onore loro salvare e la patria e la razza – Dunque mille volte meglio il delitto che la pazzia; il carceriere che mi lascia il detto latino „Cogito ergo sum" cosa che mi toglie l'alienista – Chiusa per la vita e per la vita se uscissi sospetta e oggetto

J. 115

115

Hung N°6 [illegible] in [illegible] accanto alla [illegible] delle [illegible] camere per [illegible] nella medesima.

Occorre assolutamente il loro personale intervento. E se occorrono ulteriori schiarimenti potrà rivolgersi alla Direzione dell'Ospedale Psichiatrico di Genova Quarto al S. Dott. Gardi primario del mio medico curante. È una [illegible] – Non [illegible] assolutamente [illegible]; dappoichè io sono perfettamente quanto è [illegible] alle Autorità R. Procuratore del Re di Genova e Milano e [illegible] Tribunali Civili e Penali di Milano e Genova di [illegible]

J. 116

116

Genova lì 21-7 [illegible] XIII°

Ill.mo Sig. Direttore Ospedale Psichiatrico di Genova Quarto Loco

Sig. Direttore Dott. Gardi.

mi permetto riferirmi a quanto ho accennato al Sig. dott. Risi ieri l'altro a proposito della probabilità d'intervento doloso nella pratica di ricorso che va svolgendosi con intervento personale e del Comm. Avv. Tolla, iscritto alla Cassazione di Roma, abitante in V. Donizzetti 5 Milano e P. Vittoria.

Subito in effetto dell'intendere

J. 117

117

[illegible]

√118

docter √

Dear Doctor, Please
forgive our nonchalance
regarding our last
bill. I have already
~~received~~ received
~~the intitulled~~ one
~~after say~~ but have
so far had no ~~~~ answer
~~to totil~~ I will certainly
~~Jany~~ do my best.
best ~~B~~ best wishes from
all ~~~~, 'Creatings'
~~Sincerely to all ca~~
toll Sincerely yours

139

119

[illegible] Romani quando [illegible] i popoli [illegible] non [illegible] il territorio [illegible] [illegible] i popoli [illegible] di difendere [illegible] [illegible] questo perché questi [illegible] Quindi [illegible] territorio

Ammettiamo che i popoli obbligassero l'Italia a lasciar penetrare i paesi i loro figli per venire ad essere turisti o lavoratori come l'Italia si accontenterebbe di prendere quello che viene agli altri che succederebbe? Allora [illegible] che si potrebbe far figli in quantità per il futuro [illegible]

Se va così cioè internazionalmente [illegible] ma l'uomo è nato per lavorare quindi siamo tutti gli stessi. [illegible] di lavoratori.

120

What you see in my hand Writting.
If you be kind enough to do this please let me hear From you by friday.
I have some friends who Would like to write you or come Over to see you but they Will Wait untill I hear from you. I thank you

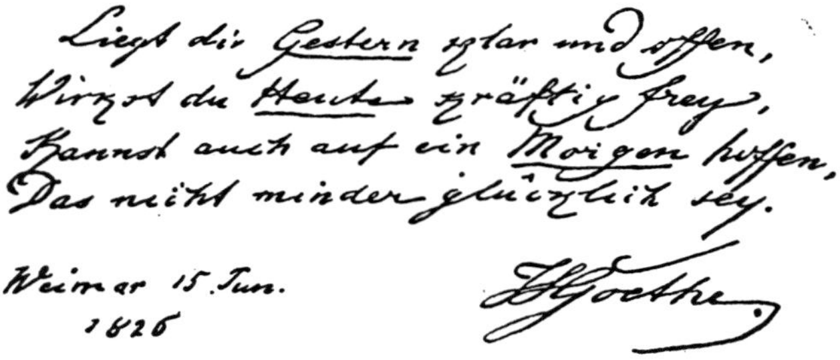
Liegt dir Gestern klar und offen,
Wirkst du Heute kräftig frey,
Kannst auch auf ein Morgen hoffen,
Das nicht minder glücklich sey.

Weimar 15. Jun.
1826

JWGoethe

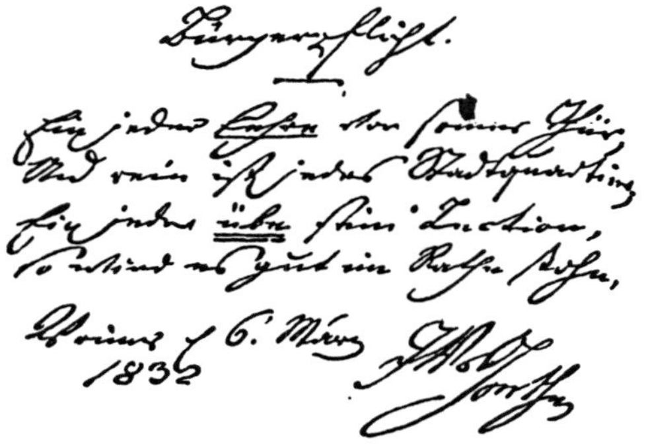
Bürgerpflicht.

Ein jeder kehre vor seiner Thür,
Und rein ist jedes Stadtquartier.
Ein jeder übe seine Lection,
So wird es gut im Rathe stohn.

Weimar d. 6. März
1832

J W v Goethe

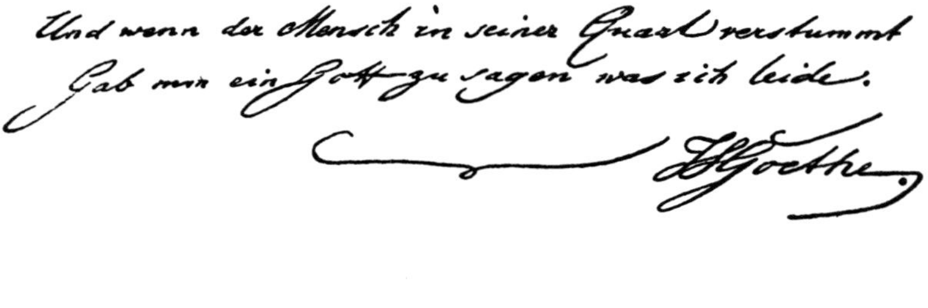
Und wenn der Mensch in seiner Qual verstummt
Gab mir ein Gott zu sagen was ich leide.

JWGoethe

Lieber geehrter Doktor, dadurch, dass
auf der Liste der Spender Ihr Vater
infolge eines Versehens ausblieb,
konnte ich Ihnen noch nicht dafür
danken, dass Sie sich an der kostbaren
Gabe gütigst beteiligten; was ich
nachträglich erspähte. Sie haben nicht
nur meinen oftmals geäußerten, sondern aller
folgenden Tage - soweit Sie mir vergangene
Tage werden - verschönt. - Eine bleibende
Erinnerung, Quelle des Genusses u.
meiner Dankbarkeit. Ihr F. Busoni

My dear Professor Perry,

It is indeed kind of you to remember me in connection with the Century Club, and I only wish I were more of a club man so that I could accept your suggestion with the feeling that I might in some occult manner fit in. As it is I so rarely go out that my election would simply be an outrage on the many waiting and anxious to get in. I have long been a member of the St. Botolph in Boston, but as a matter of fact I do not dare look my proposers in the face, as I have not set foot in the club for ages — drink a whisky at home as I am not so rigid as a club keeping off another man. and now I think you will think better of me in the end for not doing so. I need not say that the compliment is heartily appreciated and I thank you for it

With best greetings to Mrs. Perry
Sincerely yours

Edward MacDowell

Veuillez agréer, Madame, l'assurance
de ma considération la plus distinguée

Michaud

Jeudi –

Cher Monsieur

Je ne suis que pour peu de
jours à Paris; mais vous
recevrai avec plaisir.

Vous sera-t-il possible de
venir 1bis rue Vaneau,
Jeudi ou Samedi matin,
avant onze heures.

Je n'aurai que peu d'instants
à vous donner, mais serai heureux
de causer avec vous.

Bien cordialement

André Gide.

14-10-7...

Cher Monsieur,

Vous pourrez voir Cte de [illegible], marquis que j'ai vu hier, qui m'a donné l'assurance (c'est un des conseillers du [illegible] qu'il choisira). Vous feriez bien de lui écrire un mot : 157, boulevard Haussmann. Très heureux d'avoir pu vous faire plaisir, croyez, cher Monsieur, à mes sincères sympathies.

Claude Debussy.

25/8 09 — 8

4 AVENUE CARNOT

Cher Monsieur.

Voudriez-vous interpréter "Gaspard de la Nuit" au Salon d'Automne le 2 Novembre prochain? Inutile de vous dire combien je vous en serais reconnaissant. Je ne sais si vous êtes en possession de ces pièces. Ne manquez pas, dans votre réponse, de me le dire; je vous les ferai parvenir immédiatement.

Bien cordialement à vous

Maurice Ravel

Nieuw Veere
Old Greenwich, Conn.
Tel. Old Greenwich 7-1888

25 Aug 7⁴³

I am sending you an *extra* Manuscript.
Keep it.
I have a deep respect for Graphology. I knew
Dr. Saudek well. He used to come to us
in Veere. Now he is dead. Veere is gone and
if my people had studied Adolf Hitler's
ciarnograptics prior — then they would have
been warned. My sincere regards

R. Hendrik van Loon

147

BIBLIOGRAPHY

Crépieux—Jamin: Les Elements de l' écriture des canailles, Ernest Flammarion, Paris.

Klages Dr. Ludwig, Handschrift und Charakter, Johann Ambros Barth, Leipzig, 1926.

Lombroso Cesare: L'uomo delinquente, Fratelli Bocca Editori, Torino.

Pulver Dr. Max, Symbolik der Handschrift, Orell Fuessli, Zuerich 1931.

Pulver Dr. Max, Trieb und Verbrechen in der Schrift, Orell Fuessli, Zuerich 1934.

Adler Dr. Alfred, Praxis und Theorie der Individual Psychologie, J. F. Bergman, Muenchen, 1927.

Adler Dr. Alfred, The Science of Living, The World Publishing Comp. Cleveland and New York.

Freud Dr. Sigm. A general Introduction to psychoanalysis, Garden City. Publishing Comp. N. Y. C.

Jung Dr. Carl, Psychologische Typen, Rascher, Zuerich, 1925.

Jung Dr. Carl, Seelenprobleme der Gegenwart, Rascher, Zuerich, 1931.

Kretschmer Dr. Ernst, Medizinische Psychologie, George Thieme, Leipzig 1927.

Sanctus S. De Neuropsichiatria infantile, Ed. Stock, Rome.

Tanzi E. Trattato delle malatie mentali, Societa Ed. Libereario, Milano 1914-16.

Saudek Robert, Wissenchaftliche Graphologie, Drei Masken Verlag Muenchen 1926.

Saudek Robert, The Psychology of Handwriting, Doran Company N. Y. C.

Jacoby H. J. Analysis of Handwriting, George Allan and Unwin, London.

De Witt B. Lucas, Handwriting and Character, David Mc Kay Comp. Philadelphia.

Freeman Frank, The Teaching of Handwriting, London, George G. Harap.

Preyer, Prof. Dr. Psychologie des Schreibens 1895.

INDEX OF NAMES

INDEX OF SUBJECTS

RUSTON ACADEMY
Havana, Cuba

To whom it may concern:
I have known Mrs. Marcuse during her stay in Havana, for nearly a year. She is a student of graphology and has given evidence of being an expert in this field. Her characterizations are excellent and interesting. In one test of fifteen or twenty pupils whom she did not know personally, she was astonishingly accurate in her analyses of character. She has a fundamental knowledge of psychology to make her work valuable as well as interesting to teachers, parents, executives, and others whose work demands a knowledge of human traits and action.

H. H. RUSTON

JUILLIARD SCHOOL OF MUSIC, N. Y.

New York City.
I have seen several specimens of handwriting interpretations by Mme. Irene Marcuse, besides the analysis of my own script, and have found them excellent in every way.
Mme. Marcuse also specializes in many other fields of analytical work and is able to give especially musicians very valuable counsel in regard to their professional activities.

CARL FRIEDBERG. .

THE NEW YORK PSYCHOLOGY FORUM

At our last meeting, Ruth Hampton, the well known hand-writing analyst, introduced Irene Marcuse, who gave us one of the most enlightening lectures on Modern Graphology that we have ever had from our platform.

Irene Marcuse chose for her subject some of the hightligts from her book APPLIED GRAPHOLOGY, which serves as a textbook for The Hampton-Marcuse corespondence Course in Graphology. The author's insight and mastery of this progressive science was a revelation to our members and friends.

Facts were presented in the lecture similar to those obtained through Psycho-analysis yet—the method was more comprehensive and interesting because the samples of handwriting were shown on the screen, analyzed and compared with other samples.

All Hail the day when this science is more generally utalized by laymen and doctors alike

ANN KOERNING, Director

A Lt. in the United States Army who plans to use graphology for personnel work in civilian life.

Dear Miss Hampton:

The first eight lessons of the correspondence course arrived at various times during this hectic summer. . . .

Before closing, let me say, I am pleased immensely with the presentation of the course. And I enjoy your personal letters, you seem like an old friend writing to me and that helps a lot these days.

North Africa

A. P. O. 750

c|o Postmaster N. Y.

Best regards

GLENN JONES

A REGISTERED NURSE

Dear Mesdames:

After having studied the **Hampton-Marcuse** Correspondence Course I realize how much easier it is for me to understand my patients' personal problems. The lesson HANDLING THE SUPER-SENSITIVE is particularly helpful for a nurse.

You have presented something more than a course in graphology, it is a fine study of human relationship. As a registered nurse I can highly recommend this scientific course to all members of my profession.

War Relocation Hospital

Rivers, Arizona

Sincerely yours,

FLORENCE B. TEMPLE

London, England

It is a pleasure to testify to the remarkable accuracy and precision of Madame Marcuse's interpretations of the human character from handwriting. A profound understanding of the science of graphology enables her to delintate with unerring exactitude the governing motives that model character, a faculty which cannot fail to prove of inestimable service in the eradication of undesirable qualities of character, and of equal importance in the appreciation of specific capabilities in the light of their application towards success in human endeavour.

Madame Marcuse is also quick to recognise spiritual values with a full understanding of their beneficent and powerful influence on character, thus rendering her interpretations of correspondingly greater value to those wishing to give fuller expression to their individual capabilities and talents.

E. A. GREENLESS

NOW *You can learn*

How to **Analyze** *handwriting*

and earn
an income
at home!

Become a Qualified Analyst..

Learn how to discover your own aptitudes and *how to develop your personality.*

We will T E A C H Y O U how to know others; How to judge their dispositions, their motives, their likes and dislikes, their abilities and character.

The Study of this course should make your life and the relations with others more successful, and useful.

Write for detailed information how to make amazing discoveries and convert them into money.
Rates for Handwriting Analysis will be sent on request.

THE HAMPTON-MARCUSE INSTITUTE OF GRAPHOLOGY

The Modernized Correspondence Course in Graphology

200 WEST 54TH STREET   NEW YORK 19, N. Y.

IRENE MARCUZE   RUTH HAMPTON

Printed in the United States
106843LV00004B/89/A